SEX AND AMERICA'S TEENAGERS

The Alan Guttmacher Institute
New York and Washington

ACKNOWLEDGMENTS

This report builds on over a decade of research by The Alan Guttmacher Institute (AGI) and many others. It represents two years of direct research, analysis and thought by AGI staff members Patricia Donovan, senior associate for law and public policy; Jacqueline Darroch Forrest, vice president for research; Jennifer Frost, senior research associate; David J. Landry, senior research associate; and Olivia Schieffelin Nordberg, director of publications. In addition, the assistance and advice of other AGI staff were invaluable to its preparation: Daniel Daley, Beth Fredrick, Stanley K. Henshaw, Kathryn L. Kost, Cory L. Richards, Jeannie I. Rosoff and Susheela Singh. Finally, this report would not have been possible without the research assistance of Jessica W. Black and Kathryn L. Kuo, and the administrative assistance of Stefani Janicki, Joanne L. Johnson, Vanessa Kaleb, Stuart Rhoden, Marjory Ruderman and Regina Toler.

AGI is indebted to the following individuals, who reviewed the entire manuscript and made many helpful suggestions: Christine A. Bachrach, National Institute of Child Health and Human Development (NICHD); Claire Brindis, University of California–San Francisco; Arthur B. Elster, American Medical Association; Jane Johnson, Planned Parenthood Federation of America (PPFA); David Perlman, *The San Francisco Chronicle*; and Karen Pittman, Academy for Educational Development.

The counsel of two advisory panels also helped to shape the direction of the final report, and thanks are extended to those participants, listed here with their affiliation at the time of their participation: Christine A. Bachrach, NICHD; Jerry Bennett, Office of Population Affairs, U.S. Department of Health and Human Services (DHHS); Judy Bennett, Virginia Council of Churches; Robert Blum, University of Minnesota; Sarah Brown, Institute of Medicine; Sarah DePersio, Oklahoma State Department of Health; Joy Dryfoos, independent consultant; Floyd Garrett, Adolescent Family Center, Rush-Presbyterian, St. Luke's Medical Center; Olivia Golden, Children's Defense Fund; Debra Haffner, Sex Information and Education Council of the United States (SIECUS); Cheryl Hayes, independent consultant; Ann Hill, National Urban League; Marion Howard, Grady Memorial Hospital; Renee Jenkins, Howard University Hospital; Samuel Kessel, Maternal and Child Health Bureau, DHHS; Laura Colin Klein, Association of Junior Leagues; Lloyd Kolbe, Centers for Disease Control and Prevention (CDC); James Marks, CDC; James McCarthy, Center for Population and Family Health, Columbia University; Harriet Meyer, Ounce of Prevention Fund; Inca Mohammed, Young Women's Christian Association; Kristin Moore, Child Trends; Geri Peak, Center for Population Options (CPO); Margaret Pruitt-Clark, CPO; John Schlitt, Southern Center on Adolescent Pregnancy Prevention; Robert Selverstone, SIECUS; Jack Smith, CDC; Mary Sosa, National Education Association; Amy Sutnick-Plotch, Girls, Inc.; Trish Moylan Toruella, PPFA; Judy Wurtzel, U.S. Department of Education; Laurie Schwab Zabin, School of Hygiene and Public Health, Johns Hopkins University.

We acknowledge with gratitude colleagues in the field who provided us with special tabulations of data: Saul D. Hoffman, Kristin A. Moore, Christine W. Nord, Deborah Oakley, James L. Peterson and Koray Tanfer.

The research needed to produce this report was supported in large part by the Carnegie Corporation of New York and the Charles Stewart Mott Foundation. The Marion Cohen Memorial Foundation and the General Services Foundation helped to support its production and distribution.

ISBN: 0-939253-34-8

The Alan Guttmacher Institute

120 Wall Street
New York, New York 10005

1120 Connecticut Avenue, N.W.
Washington, D.C. 20036

Table of Contents

Summary

Over the last century, the transition from childhood to adulthood has been radically, and probably irrevocably, altered. Many of the traditional markers of adulthood, such as full-time employment, economic independence, marriage and childbearing, now generally occur at later ages than in past generations. At the same time, young people initiate sexual intercourse much earlier than in the past, and long before they marry. Most adolescents today begin to have intercourse in their middle to late teens. More than half of women and almost three-quarters of men have had intercourse before their 18th birthday; in the mid-1950s, by contrast, just over a quarter of women were sexually experienced by age 18. As sex has become more common at younger ages, differences in sexual activity between gender, racial, socioeconomic and religious groups have narrowed considerably.

Despite these trends, teenagers generally do not initiate sexual intercourse as early as most adults believe. Nor do all teenagers have sex. Although the likelihood of having intercourse increases steadily with age, nearly 20% of adolescents do not have intercourse at all during their teenage years. Moreover, many of the youngest teenagers who have had intercourse report that they were forced to do so.

Most adolescents who are sexually experienced try to protect themselves and their partners from the negative consequences of sex—namely, sexually transmitted diseases (STDs) and unintended pregnancy—even the first time they have intercourse. Two-thirds of adolescents use some method of contraception—usually the male condom—the first time they have sex, and between 72% and 84% of teenage women use a method of contraception on an ongoing basis. Although their contraceptive use is often less than perfect, a large majority of these young people succeed in avoiding unintended pregnancy. In fact, teenagers use contraceptives as effectively as or even better than adults; adolescents have lower rates of unintended pregnancy, for example, than unmarried method users in their early 20s.

For adolescents who are not effective contraceptive users or who do not use a method, the consequences can be serious, especially for young women. Every year, 3 million teenagers acquire an STD, which can imperil their ability to have children or lead to serious health problems, such as cancer and infection with the AIDS virus. In addition, 1 million teenage women become pregnant every year, the vast majority unintentionally. Pregnancy rates among sexually experienced teenagers have declined substantially over the last two decades, but because the proportion of teenagers who have had intercourse has grown, the overall teenage pregnancy rate has increased. Older teenagers and adolescents who are poor or black are more likely to get pregnant than are their younger, more advantaged and white counterparts.

Teenagers who become pregnant almost always have an abortion or give birth and raise the child themselves; placing a child for adoption is rare. About half of adolescent pregnancies end in birth, slightly over a third in abortion and the rest in miscarriage. The way in which adolescent women resolve their pregnancies is determined largely by their socioeconomic status. Young women who come from advantaged families generally have abortions. Childbearing, on the other hand, is concentrated among teenagers who are poor and low-income; in fact, more than 80% of young women who give birth fall into one of these income categories.

Young mothers tend not only to be disadvantaged economically, educationally and socially at the time of their child's birth, but also to be at risk of falling further behind their more advantaged peers who postponed childbearing to obtain more education and to advance their careers. Teenage mothers, for example, obtain less education and have lower future family incomes than young women who delay their first birth. Many are poor later in life, and while it is clear that their initial disadvantaged background is a major reason for their subsequent poverty, it is also clear that early childbearing has a lasting impact on the lives and future opportunities of young mothers and of their children.

Current trends in sexual behavior

among U.S. teenagers are similar to trends both among U.S. adults and among teenage and adult women and men in other countries. For example, the proportion of births to U.S. women in their 20s that were out of wedlock has increased fourfold in the last 20 years. In fact, adult women, not teenagers, account for large majorities of the unintended pregnancies, abortions and out-of-wedlock births that occur each year. Furthermore, even though nearly 70% of births to adolescents occur outside of marriage, teenagers account for a smaller proportion of out-of-wedlock births today than they did in 1970.

If adults are going to help teenagers avoid the outcomes of sex that are clearly negative—STDs, unintended pregnancies, abortions and out-of-wedlock births—they must accept the reality of adolescent sexual activity and deal with it directly and honestly. Certain interventions are needed by all teenagers. All adolescents, for example, need sex education that teaches them communication skills that will help them postpone sex until they are ready and that provides information about specific methods to prevent pregnancy and STDs. All young people also need clear and frequent reminders from their parents, the media and other sources about the importance of behaving responsibly when they initiate sexual intercourse. Sexually experienced teenagers need accessible contraceptive services, STD screening and treatment, and prenatal and abortion services, regardless of their income status.

As important as these interventions are, they do not address the entrenched poverty that is a major cause of early childbearing among disadvantaged teenage women. Only when their poverty is alleviated, and these young women—and their partners—have access to good schools and jobs and come to believe that their futures can be brighter, is real change in their sexual behavior and its outcomes likely to occur.

Other industrialized countries are also dealing with issues related to adolescent sexual activity, but teenage pregnancy, abortion and childbearing are bigger problems in this country, for several reasons: Elsewhere in the industrialized world, there is a greater openness about sexual relationships; the media reinforce the importance of using contraceptives to avoid pregnancy and STDs; and contraceptives are generally more accessible to teenagers because reproductive health care is better integrated into general health services. We can learn from the successes of other countries, as well as from programs in this country that have had a positive impact on teenagers' initiation of sexual intercourse and contraceptive use, to better help young people avoid being adversely and needlessly affected by sexual behavior.

If adults are going to help teenagers avoid the outcomes of sex that are clearly negative, they must accept the reality of adolescent sexual activity and deal with it directly and honestly.

Rites of Passage

Sex is part of virtually everyone's life. For adults and teenagers alike, having sex can have positive or negative consequences. On the positive side, it can bring pleasure; draw a couple closer together; and lead to a desired pregnancy and wanted children. In different circumstances, however, having sex can engender a sense of shame or guilt; push a couple apart; raise unrealistic expectations of further commitment and marriage; or be a form of abuse. It can also result in an unintended pregnancy or infection with a sexually transmitted disease (STD), including human immunodeficiency virus (HIV).

Ironically, while sex is one of the most intimate of behaviors, sexual references and innuendos are openly and widely used to entertain and to sell products. Moreover, many people care intensely about the sexual behavior of others. We discuss, argue about and even legislate boundaries of appropriate sexual behavior.

Delaying sexual intimacy; achieving lasting, loving relationships; and understanding and accepting the responsibilities and costs that accompany sexual activity—these are difficult under the best circumstances, but can be especially hard for adolescents.

For teenagers and their families, as well as for society as a whole, adolescence is a period of growth, challenge and opportunity. It is a time of testing and experimentation, as young people adopt new roles and an independent identity. Over time, society's definitions of childhood and adulthood have changed, however; so, too, have the timing, length and context of adolescence.

Young people represent the country's hopes for a brighter future. Yet, the world in which teenagers grow up today is very different from that of their parents' and grandparents' youth, and many adults are concerned about the pressures on adolescents. Perhaps no area is of greater concern, has more implications for an individual's life and future well-being or is more fraught with ambiguity than sexual relationships.

The Turning Point

Society has little tolerance for emerging sexuality during childhood, but accepts—indeed, expects—that adults have intercourse. Consensus evaporates, however, on the point in an individual's life at which society should shift from treating sex as inappropriate to considering it acceptable behavior.

In past generations, the issue was fairly easily resolved. Marriage marked the turning point. Historically, at least for young women, the physical capability to have sex and reproduce typically did not occur until the mid-teenage years. The social transition of marriage and the assumption of other adult responsibilities, such as employment, establishing one's own household and having children, commonly took place soon thereafter.

Sexual activity among adolescents has always been common; but in the past, it was closely linked to marriage, especially for young women. Sex outside marriage certainly occurred, but it was not considered a major social problem, in large part because its chief negative consequence—unintended pregnancy—was generally dealt with by marriage, or by clandestine adoption or abortion.

Diverging Transitions

Times have changed. Over the last century, puberty has slowly moved to earlier ages, and so has the initiation of sexual activity. Most adolescents now begin to have intercourse in their middle or late teens—long before they marry (Figure 1, page 7). Furthermore, as sex has become more common at younger ages, behavior of various subgroups of the population has converged: Differences in sexual activity between gender, racial, socioeconomic and religious groups have substantially narrowed.

While sex now occurs at earlier ages, young people reach other traditional markers of adulthood, such as full-time employment and economic independence, at later ages, because more education is needed for today's jobs. Moreover, education and employment have become accepted, almost required paths to adulthood for young women, as well as for young men. Rather than considering these responsibilities alternatives to marriage and motherhood, young women pursue them and the more traditional ones simultaneously.[1] As the ages at which young people complete their education and begin full-time employment have risen, and as work has become an ongoing part of most women's lives, marriage and parenthood have tended to occur at older ages, especially for women. Moreover, a small but increasing proportion of adults never marry.[2]

Defining the "Problem"

Although young people's sexual behavior today is broadly seen as problematic, there is no consensus on exactly what the "problem" is. About one-third of adults think that sexual activity in and of itself is the problem because sex outside marriage is morally wrong.[3] Most adults, however, do not think that sex prior to marriage is always wrong; in fact, some believe that sexual activity under certain conditions is normal, healthy behavior even for adolescents.[4] For them, adolescent sexual behavior is a matter of concern largely because of the possible negative outcomes—namely, unintended pregnancy and STDs. The degree of concern generally varies, however, according to the age and maturity of the young people involved; sexual activity, or even pregnancy, among those in their late teens raises far less concern than does sex among very young adolescents. For some adults, the primary problem is the cost to society of providing services, particularly welfare, to help young people who are poor deal with the demands of early parenthood.

This lack of clarity has been translated into public policy and program development. Heretofore, much of the energy directed at addressing adolescent sexual activity has been focused either on trying to convince young people to delay the initiation of sex until "later"—ideally, until they are married—or on providing remedial medical and social services to teenagers who are pregnant or parents so they will have healthy babies and stay in school. The first approach appears to be based on the premise that young people can be isolated from the worldwide trend toward separation of sex from marriage. The second seems to assume that the only effective actions society can take are remedial ones after young women get

BIG CHANGES

The interval for women between puberty and marriage rose from 7.2 years in 1890 to 11.8 years in 1988; for men in 1988, it was 12.5 years.

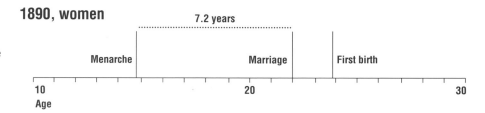

1890, women

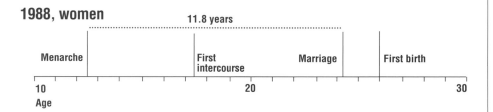

1988, women

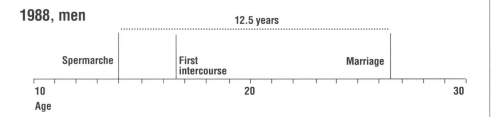

1988, men

Sources: Menarche, 1890: E. G. Wyshak and R. E. Frisch, "Evidence for a Secular Trend in Age of Menarche," *New England Journal of Medicine*, **306**:1033–1035, 1982. **First marriage, 1890:** U.S. Bureau of the Census, "Marital Status and Living Arrangements: March, 1990," *Current Population Reports*, Series P-20, No. 450, 1991, Table A, p. 1. **First birth, 1890:** National Center for Health Statistics, *Fertility Tables for Birth Cohorts by Color, United States, 1917–73*, Public Health Service, Rockville, Md., 1976, Table 6A, p. 145. **Menarche, first intercourse and first birth and first marriage, 1988:** J. D. Forrest, "Timing of Reproductive Life Stages," *Obstetrics and Gynecology*, **82**:105–111, 1993, Table 3. **Spermarche, 1988:** E. Atwater, *Adolescence*, third ed. Prentice-Hall, Englewood Cliffs, N.J., 1992, p. 63.

Notes: Menarche is the beginning of menstruation in females. **Spermarche** is the beginning of sperm production in males. The data for the different time periods are not totally comparable. For 1890, age at first marriage is calculated in the usual manner as the age by which 50% of the ever-married population had married. (Median age at marriage in 1890 would be higher if it were calculated for the total population.) The 1890 first-birth figure is calculated from the 1917 birth cohort; the 1890 number is unavailable, but it is estimated to be lower. For 1988, the median ages at menarche, spermarche, first intercourse, marriage and first birth are calculated as the age by which 50% of the total female (or male) population in 1988 had experienced the event.

Data points: 1890, women: age at menarche, 14.8; marriage, 22.0; first birth, 23.8. **1988, women:** age at menarche, 12.5; first intercourse, 17.4; marriage, 24.3; first birth, 26.0. **1988, men:** age at spermarche, 14.0; first intercourse, 16.6; marriage, 26.5.

FIGURE 1

pregnant and are about to become mothers. To be sure, there have been important efforts to help teenagers behave responsibly if they do become sexually active. Family planning clinics, for example, have become a critical source of contraceptive services for teenagers. Meanwhile, school-based and school-linked clinics and, more recently, condom distribution programs in schools seek to make the means to prevent pregnancy and STDs more accessible, and virtually all school systems provide some sex education.

Yet, these efforts have been insufficient. Although sex education is widespread, it often includes minimal instruction about pregnancy and STD prevention. Relatively few school-based and school-linked clinics are in operation around the country, and only a third of them dispense contraceptives; similarly, only a small number of condom distribution programs are in existence.[5] Family planning clinics are far more numerous, but they can help only those teenagers who come in for care.

Dealing with Reality

It is clear that most young women and men will become sexually active during their teenage years, or very soon thereafter. Should society continue to focus its efforts on changing that fact, thinking that young people need—or deserve—only the admonition not to have sex until they marry in their middle or late 20s? Or is it time for society to accept the reality of young people's lives, and to concentrate on giving teenagers the information, guidance and services they need—both to withstand pressure from their peers and the media to have sex too soon, and to have healthy, responsible and mutually protective relationships when they do become sexually active?

Meeting the varied needs of today's teenagers requires a thorough understanding of the challenges that face young people, the ways that adolescents meet those challenges and the impact on those who are not successful in doing so. This report of The Alan Guttmacher Institute (AGI) seeks to provide that understanding. The report begins with an overview of the world in which adolescents are growing up. It then examines trends in teenage sexual activity and adolescents' efforts to protect themselves and their partners from the negative consequences of sex, and describes the incidence and outcomes of sexually transmitted infections and pregnancy among teenagers. The report also looks at the effects of programmatic and policy interventions that have tried to influence adolescent sexual behavior and ameliorate its negative effects. In conclusion, it discusses how adults individually and society in general can more effectively help young people become healthy, responsible and competent adults.

The Context of Adolescents' Lives

Adolescents today live in a country that is more diverse than the one their parents knew as teenagers. Increased mobility and communication have made the gap between rich and poor more visible, and tensions between racial and ethnic communities more apparent. Some young people, especially blacks, encounter racism and prejudice, just as their parents and grandparents have. Many teenagers of Hispanic descent, meanwhile, were born outside the United States; adolescence may therefore be a more difficult transition for them than for native-born teenagers.[6]

Young people increasingly spend part or all of their youth in single-parent families, families with two working parents or "blended" families; as a consequence, they tend to have less-consistent adult assistance and supervision. In addition, adolescents and their families are often less tied to their communities than were past generations.

More education is needed by young people today to get a good job, but even a college degree is no guarantee of achieving economic independence and job security. Violence is commonplace in many communities. And AIDS has cast the threat of death over sexual relationships at a time when sexual messages pervade virtually all aspects of American life.

In sum, it is a confusing, and at times even frightening, period to be a teenager in America, and to be a parent of a teenager.

Shared Values

Despite their experimentation and apparent rejection of adult values, adolescents share many of their parents' goals and perspectives, including values that affect their sexual and reproductive lives. For example:

♦Most teenagers consider responsibility, honesty, self-respect and hard work important values.[7]

♦Nearly all adolescents believe that education is important.[8]

♦More than eight in 10 teenagers expect to marry, and more than seven in 10 would like to have children.[9]

♦The overwhelming majority of young people say their most important goals include having a good marriage and family life, giving their children better opportunities than they had, and finding purpose and meaning in life.[10]

♦ The vast majority of adolescents have a sense of religious commitment.[11]

♦Like adults, about a third of young people think sex before marriage is always a mistake. Teenagers rarely think premarital sex is immoral; rather, they believe young people should abstain from sex because of the risk of getting AIDS or becoming pregnant.[12]

While they may share their parents' values, many teenagers are unable to achieve their goals because economic and social disadvantage impedes their chances of getting a good education, finding a good job and living in a safe neighborhood with both biological parents.

Fractured Society

A large proportion of the country's 24 million teenagers[13] live in families that have difficulty providing such basics as food, clothing and shelter.[14]

♦Nearly 40% of women and men aged 15–19 are poor or low-income.

♦Hispanic and black teenagers are substantially more likely than white youth to be economically disadvantaged (Figure 2, page 12).

High levels of poverty among children and youth from racial and ethnic minorities, combined with persistent de facto segregation in housing and schools, mean that some adolescents, especially blacks, grow up in economic and racial ghettos, where alienation often thrives and education and marriage may not be the norm.[15]

Disparities in Education

More than eight in 10 young people graduate from high school by age 20, but there are large differences in educational attainment by income group and, among those who are poor or low-income, by racial and ethnic group[16] (Figure 3, page 13). Less education compounds the economic disadvantage of poor youth and of racial and ethnic minorities by making it less likely that these young people will

Definitions

Adolescence
"Adolescence" is generally viewed as being synonymous with the teenage years—that is, ages 13–19. Where feasible, this report includes information for age-groups 10–14, 15–17, 18–19 and 20–24, because it is increasingly clear that younger and older teenagers differ in experience and behavior, and that for some young people, transitions historically associated with adolescence occur before age 13 or after age 19.

Sexual activity
In this report, "sexual activity" refers to heterosexual intercourse, although this definition encompasses only one aspect of sexual behavior among heterosexuals and excludes homosexual relationships entirely. (Most national data on sexual behavior are limited to heterosexual relationships.)The term "sexually experienced" refers to those people who have ever had heterosexual intercourse.

Pregnancy
"Pregnancy" generally refers to an individual woman's state of being pregnant regardless of whether the outcome of the conception is a birth, abortion or miscarriage.

Race and ethnicity
Race and ethnicity are cross-classified to create three major categories: black non-Hispanic, Hispanic, and white non-Hispanic and other non-Hispanic. Most surveys are not large enough to provide reliable data for smaller groups, such as Asians or Native Americans. These groups are included in the third category. Throughout this report, the three labels have been condensed to "black," "Hispanic" and "white." Information is often presented by race and ethnicity because it is not available by income status; race and ethnicity are used to reflect income status because blacks and Hispanics are so much more likely than whites to be poor.

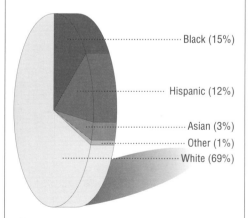

Black (15%)
Hispanic (12%)
Asian (3%)
Other (1%)
White (69%)

Total population aged 15–19, 1990: 17,754,000

Source: U.S. Bureau of the Census, *General Population Characteristics, United States 1990*, CP-1-1, U.S. Government Printing Office, 1992, Table 25, p. 34.

find stable, well-paying jobs. In turn, the poor job prospects for black men, relative to those for whites and for black women, can be a disincentive for young black men to invest in education.[17]

Changes in Family Structure

Poor and low-income teenagers and those from racial and ethnic minorities are more likely than higher income adolescents and white youths to live in families that do not include both biological parents[18] (Figure 4, page 14).

♦ Among young women aged 14, for example, those who are poor are twice as likely as those who are higher income to live in a family headed by their mother.

♦ Similarly, black adolescents of that age are about three times as likely as their white counterparts to live in a family headed by their mother.

Even so, the onetime norm of a stable, two-parent family is becoming less common across all racial and income groups. Between the late 1950s and mid-1980s, the proportion of 14-year-old women who did not live with both parents rose from 21% to 38%; most of these young women lived with their unmarried mother.[19] The connection between single-parent households and low income reflects, at least in part, the fact that working women earn lower wages than men, and the fact that unpaid child support and divorce settlements fail to provide adequate income for the custodial parent.[20]

While single parents can and do give their children love and support, providing adequate supervision for their children may be more difficult than it is for two parents.[21] Dealing with instability associated with changes in one's family status, and especially with the personal and financial disruption caused by divorce, may be especially difficult for teenagers, who are forming their own perceptions of adult relationships.[22] Moreover, children living with an unmarried parent or with a parent who remarries may be aware that their parent is having sex, since roughly two-thirds of formerly married women and men aged 20–44 are sexually active.[23] Research suggests that these adolescents may view the implications of nonmarital childbearing less negatively than others.[24]

Violence and Risk Taking

Violent crime is common in the United States, especially in large cities.[25] Violence or the threat of violence makes many adolescents fearful.[26]

♦ More than a third of 13–17-year-olds say they are afraid to walk alone at night.

♦ Almost as many fear for their safety while in school, with good reason: In 1988, about 10% of these young people had been physically assaulted or beaten at school within the past 12 months.

♦ Some 2 million cases of child neglect and abuse, including sexual abuse, are reported annually;[27] adolescents are more likely than younger children to be abused.[28]

Violent Death. Death among adolescents is rare, and is usually the result of an accident.[29] But of those teenagers who do die, nearly a third are murdered or commit suicide.

♦ The risk of a violent death is especially high for young black men: Almost half of black men aged 15–19 who die are murdered (Figure 5, page 15). The chance that a black male teenager will die is more than a third again as high as the risk for young white men; the likelihood of being murdered is almost 10 times as high.

♦ Black teenage women are four times more likely to be murdered than their white counterparts.

♦ Suicide, on the other hand, is more common among white teenagers, who are twice as likely as blacks to take their own life.

The fear of violence and its consequences may contribute to a willingness among young people to take risks. Some experts, for example, report that inner-city, black teenage women fear that young black men's chances of early death or imprisonment are so high that they should grab at the chance for love and children while they are young.[30]

Drug Use and Other Risky Behaviors. Many people experiment with smoking, drinking or drug use at some time during adolescence, but most concern is focused on those who engage heavily in such behaviors.

♦ About 4% of 14–15-year-olds and 13% of 16–18-year-olds are heavy smokers.[31]

♦ More than one-third of students in

grades 9–12 are heavy drinkers.[32]

♦ About 14% of high school students have used marijuana within the last 30 days. High school seniors are more likely to engage in drug use and drinking than are younger students.[33]

♦ By 12th grade, 8% of young people have tried cocaine.[34]

Often, there is considerable overlap in high-risk behaviors. Teenagers who abuse drugs, for example, are much more likely than others to also drink and smoke heavily, drop out of school, have sex at a young age and experience early childbearing.[35]

Teenagers who engage in risky behaviors may have more difficulty in and less support for handling the stresses and tasks of adolescence, may be depressed or may have a greater tolerance or need for risk taking. These young people may need special guidance, mental health interventions and support services.

Extended Transitions

Many of the transitions that have historically occurred during the teenage years, including the move from school to full-time employment and the establishment of one's own household, now extend into the early 20s and beyond.

Entering the Labor Force. At the beginning of their teenage years, virtually all young women and men are in school; by their late teens and early 20s, however, the majority of young people are in the labor force, although some continue to go to school and work at the same time[36] (Figure 6, page 16). Part-time work has been suggested as a useful step in learning skills and attitudes that will help in the transition to full-time employment;[37] at the same time, a job may interfere with a young person's education, if he or she begins working at too young an age or works too many hours a week.[38] Hispanics and blacks are less likely than whites to combine working with going to school, perhaps because they encounter greater difficulty finding employment.[39]

Young people often have to stay in school longer to achieve the same employment opportunities their parents had.[40] Whether this is because more education is actually needed to perform these jobs or

because educational achievement is used as a screen for scarce employment opportunities, there are fewer and poorer employment possibilities for those who have not completed high school, and even for those who have finished high school but have gone no further. Median income of women and men aged 18–24 who have had at least four years of college is about $20,000 and $23,000, respectively—roughly 50% higher than that of young people who have only a high school diploma.[41]

Moving Out. For many young people, living apart from one's parents is the true mark of reaching adulthood. It signals the end of close parental supervision and responsibility, and exposes teenagers to new people, perspectives and ideas. In their late teens and early 20s, many young people go off to college; enroll in the armed forces; or live with groups of friends, a spouse or an unmarried partner. Yet, almost half of 20–24-year-olds live at home with their parents.[42]

Pervasive Messages About Sex

Young people are bombarded with sexual images and messages in advertising, entertainment and virtually all other aspects of their lives. Television shows are filled with sexual embraces and innuendo, but say little about responsible sexual behavior (such as contraceptive use) or the potential negative consequences of sexual activity.[43] Movies, music videos and rap music tend to be even more sexually explicit. Even in presumably protective environments, such as schools, teenagers are often surrounded by sexual messages.[44]

♦ More than eight in 10 public school students in grades 8–11, for example, say they have been the recipient of unwelcome sexual comments or advances, usually from another student (Figure 7, page 17).

♦ At the same time, nearly six in 10 students report that they have subjected someone else at school to unwanted sexual comments or actions. Many students who engage in such behavior consider it a normal part of school life or a way to get a date.

Inadequate Information. AIDS has brought the specter of debilitating disease and death to sexual activity. Teenagers are worried about AIDS; more than half

Unintended pregnancy
"Unintended pregnancy" refers to a pregnancy that occurs at a time when a woman had wanted to postpone childbearing or had not wanted to have a child at all. Measurement of unintended pregnancy is an inexact science and does not capture different levels of motivation to avoid pregnancy or changing commitment to childbearing after pregnancy occurs.

At risk of unintended pregnancy
A woman is considered "at risk of unintended pregnancy" if she has had intercourse in the last three months, but does not want to have a baby at the present time, although she would be physically able to become pregnant were she and her partner to use no method of contraception.

Sexually transmitted disease (STD)
A sexually transmitted disease is an infection that can be passed from one person to another during sexual intimacy. Transmission most often occurs through vaginal intercourse, but many STDs can also be spread through oral or anal sex. In the past, STDs were generally called venereal diseases; today, they are sometimes referred to as sexually transmitted infections or reproductive tract infections.

Poor, low-income, higher income
"Poor" is defined as having annual family income at or below the poverty level set by the federal government. In 1992, the federal poverty level for a single person was $7,143. For a two-person family, it was $9,137; for a family of four, it was $14,335. In this report, "low-income" is defined as 100%–199% of the federal poverty level. For a single person, this would range from $7,143 to $14,285. "Higher income" is defined as 200% or more of poverty; for a single person, this would be the equivalent of $14,286 or more. Throughout this report, information that is not available by income status is often presented by race and ethnicity.

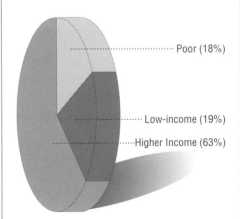

Poor (18%)

Low-income (19%)

Higher Income (63%)

Total population aged 15–19, 1992: 16,569,000

Source: AGI tabulations of data from the March 1992 Current Population Survey.

Note: Poverty data in the 1992 Current Population Survey refer to total income in 1991.

Throughout this report, whenever possible, the latest available data as of fall 1993 were used.

of young people aged 13–17 think AIDS is the country's most urgent health problem.[45] Despite their concerns and our culture's heavy emphasis on sex, many teenagers believe they have too little accurate information about sex[46] (Figure 8, page 18).

Most young people first learn about sex from their friends, their school or the media, rather than their parents.[47] Yet, many teenagers think parents are the most accurate source of information and would like to talk to their parents more about sex.[48]

♦ One-third of 15-year-old women say neither parent has talked to them about how pregnancy occurs; about half say a parent has not discussed birth control methods or STDs with them.[49]

♦ Communication does not appear to improve appreciably as teenagers get older.[50]

♦ Young men probably get even less information from their parents than do adolescent women.

The overwhelming majority of adolescents receive some sex education, including information about birth control methods and STD prevention, through programs offered in schools, churches or some other organization.[51] Frequently, though, these programs are limited in both scope and duration. School programs, for example, typically emphasize sexual facts and knowledge, rather than skills and interpersonal communication and contraceptive decision making. In addition, they average a total of only five hours of instruction on birth control and six hours on STDs between grades 7 and 12, and a large proportion of sex education teachers feel constrained in what information they can present on these topics. Furthermore, instruction often comes after teenagers have become sexually experienced.[52]

♦♦♦♦

Many teenagers are growing up in poor or low-income families, without access to a good education, good jobs and safe neighborhoods, but all teenagers, whether they are rich or poor, are exposed to an almost constant barrage of sexual messages and innuendos. Yet, despite society's fears about AIDS and adults' frequent bemoaning of high levels of teenage pregnancy and childbearing, adolescents hear relatively little about the importance of responsible sexual behavior and of protecting oneself and one's partner from the risk of pregnancy, HIV and other STDs. In view of the current level of adolescent sexual activity, the failure or inability of parents, schools, other institutions and the media to provide teenagers with the information and skills they need to avoid the negative outcomes of sex not only is sad, it is indefensible.

HAVES AND HAVE-NOTS

Many young people are growing up in families with very limited financial resources: Roughly two-thirds of blacks and Hispanics are poor or low-income.

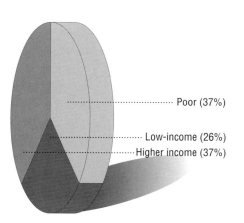

Blacks aged 15–19, 1992: 2,573,000

- Poor (37%)
- Low-income (26%)
- Higher income (37%)

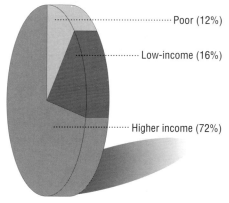

Whites aged 15–19, 1992: 12,131,000

- Poor (12%)
- Low-income (16%)
- Higher income (72%)

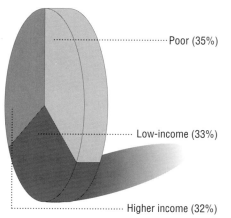

Hispanics aged 15–19, 1992: 1,865,000

- Poor (35%)
- Low-income (33%)
- Higher income (32%)

Source: AGI tabulations of data from the March 1992 Current Population Survey.

Note: Poverty data in the 1992 Current Population Survey refer to total income in 1991.

FIGURE 2

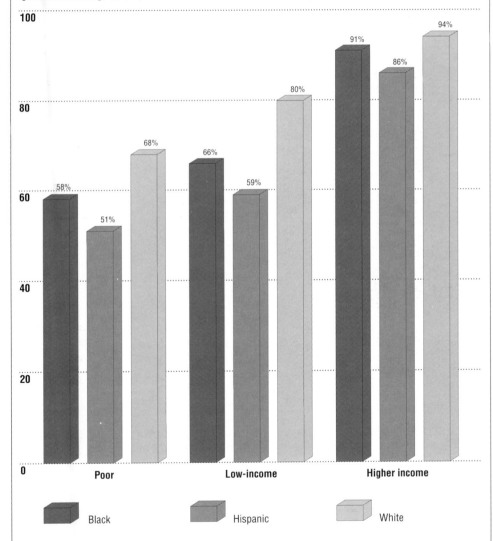

EDUCATIONAL DISADVANTAGES

Young people who are economically disadvantaged and, within income groups, those who are black or Hispanic, are less likely than others to graduate from high school on schedule.

% of 20-year-olds who have graduated from high school, 1992

Legend: Black, Hispanic, White

Poor: Black 58%, Hispanic 51%, White 68%
Low-income: Black 66%, Hispanic 59%, White 80%
Higher income: Black 91%, Hispanic 86%, White 94%

Source: AGI tabulations of data from the March 1992 Current Population Survey.

FIGURE 3

DIVERSE FAMILIES

Many young women, especially those who are poor
or are black, live with only one biological parent.

% of 14-year-old women not living with both biological parents, 1983–1987

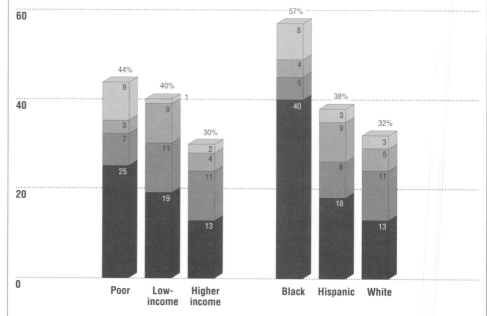

Living arrangement

 Mother only

 Father only, or father and stepmother

 Mother and stepfather

 Neither parent

Source: AGI tabulations of data from the 1988 National
Survey of Family Growth.

Notes: Data are for women who were aged 15–19 at time of
survey and refer to their living arrangements when they were
aged 14, i.e., in 1983–1987. "Parent" refers to biological status.

FIGURE 4

UNSAFE COMMUNITIES

Concerns about violence can add instability and fear to young people's lives.
Almost half of all young black men who die each year are murdered.

Deaths per 100,000 15–19-year-olds, 1988

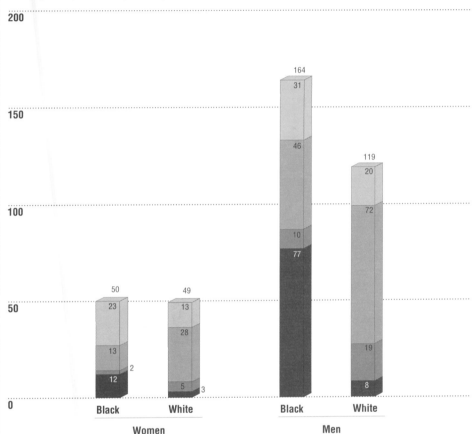

Cause of death

 Homicide   Suicide   Accidents   Other

Source: National Center for Health Statistics, *Vital Statistics of the United States, 1988. Vol. II—Mortality.* Part A, U.S. Government Printing Office, Washington, D.C., 1991, Table I-9, pp. 14, 36–37.

Note: In this figure, the terms "black" and "white" refer to race; Hispanics are categorized by race, not ethnicity. Because death is a rare event among young people, this scale is expressed per 100,000 persons, not per 1,000.

FIGURE 5

It is a confusing, and at times even frightening, period to be a teenager in America, and to be a parent of a teenager.

Young people often have to stay in school longer to achieve the same employment opportunities their parents had.

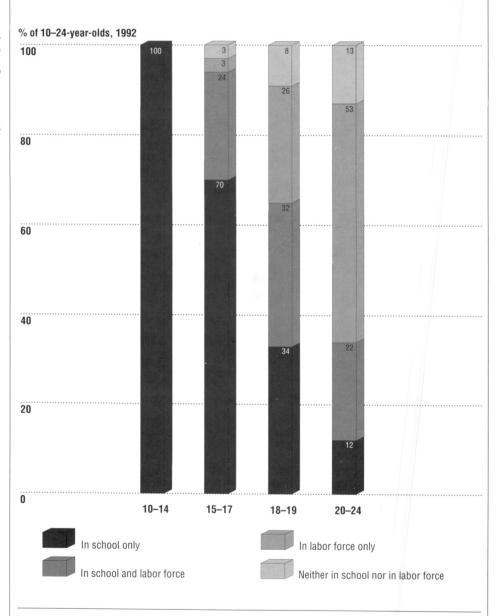

LONG TRANSITION FROM SCHOOL TO WORK

For many young people, the transition from school to labor force extends well into their 20s.

% of 10–24-year-olds, 1992

In school only

In labor force only

In school and labor force

Neither in school nor in labor force

Source: AGI tabulations of data from the March 1992 Current Population Survey.

Note: "In labor force" includes those employed and those unemployed but actively seeking work.

FIGURE 6

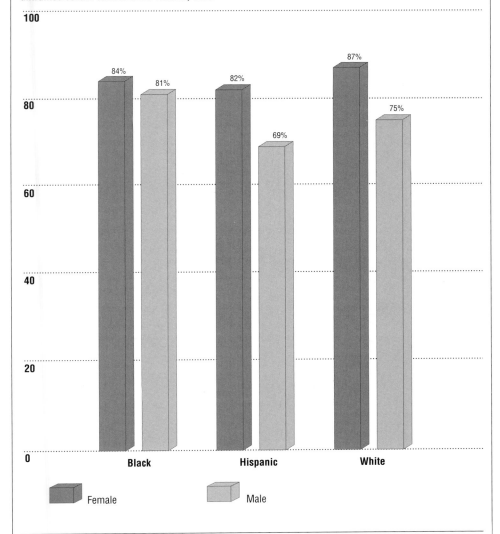

SEXUAL PRESSURE AT SCHOOL

Most teenagers—women more than men—report receiving
unwanted sexual comments or actions at school.

**% of students in grades 8–11 reporting
unwanted sexual comments or actions, 1993**

Black   84% (Female)   81% (Male)
Hispanic   82% (Female)   69% (Male)
White   87% (Female)   75% (Male)

■ Female   □ Male

Source: Harris/Scholastic Research, *Hostile Hallways: The AAUW Survey on Sexual Harassment in America's Schools,* American Association of University Women Educational Foundation, Washington, D.C., 1993, p. 7.

Note: Sexual comments or actions include experiences during school-related times. Students were asked whether they had been subjected to one or more of seven types of actions involving physical contact, from "touched, grabbed or pinched you in a sexual way" to "forced you to do something sexual, other than kissing," and seven actions involving no physical contact, including sexual comments, jokes or gestures, and being "flashed" or "mooned."

FIGURE 7

The failure to provide teen-agers with the information and skills they need to avoid the negative outcomes of sex not only is sad, it is indefensible.

TOO LITTLE INFORMATION

Almost half of 15–19-year-olds think the average young person today does not have enough accurate information about sex and reproduction.

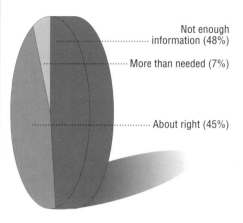

Not enough information (48%)

More than needed (7%)

About right (45%)

Women and men aged 15–19, 1988: 18,496,000

Sources: Women: AGI tabulations of data from the 1988 National Survey of Family Growth. **Men:** AGI tabulations of data from the 1988 National Survey of Adolescent Males. **Total population:** U.S. Bureau of the Census, "U.S. Population Estimates, by Age, Sex, Race and Hispanic Origin: 1980–1991," *Current Population Reports,* Series P-25, No. 1095, 1993, Table 1, p. 10.

FIGURE 8

Sex Among Teenagers

Although sex is common among teenagers, it is not as widespread, and does not begin as early, as most adults believe. Adults generally think that teenagers start having sexual intercourse before they turn 16,[53] but few very young adolescents are sexually experienced. In fact, more than half of teenagers are virgins until they are at least 17.[54] Furthermore, while the likelihood of having intercourse increases steadily with age, nearly 20% of adolescents do not have sex at all during their teenage years[55] (Figure 9, page 19).

Increasing Prevalence of Sex

Nevertheless, a greater proportion of teenagers have sex today than did so in recent decades. More than half of women and almost three-quarters of men have had intercourse before their 18th birthday; in the mid-1950s, by contrast, just over a quarter of women under age 18 were sexually experienced[56] (comparable information for men is not available for that time period) (Figure 10, page 20). At each age between 15 and 20, higher proportions of teenage men and women are sexually experienced today than were in the early 1970s (Figures 11 and 12, pages 22 and 23).

Later Marriage

At the same time, women and men who marry today do so 3–4 years later than did their counterparts in the 1950s[57] (Figure 13, page 24).

♦ In 1992, only 8% of 19-year-olds—12% of women and 3% of men—were married.[58]

♦ Hispanics are the most likely, and blacks the least likely, to marry in their teenage years; 24% of 19-year-old Hispanic women are married, compared with only 12% of whites and 5% of blacks in that age-group.[59]

Although a smaller proportion of young people are marrying, a larger share are cohabiting outside marriage.[60] In 1988, just over 3% of women aged 15–19 were married; about 4% were living in a cohabiting relationship; and another 4% had broken up a cohabiting relationship and remained unmarried.[61]

Sex Outside Marriage

As a result of these trends, 96% of women who have intercourse as teenagers are unmarried when they first have sex.[62]

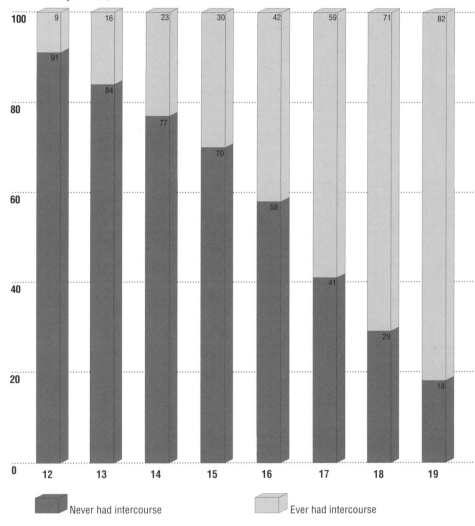

INTERCOURSE AND AGE

Sex is rare among very young teenagers, but common in the later teenage years.

% of 12–19-year-olds, 1988

Never had intercourse   Ever had intercourse

Age	12	13	14	15	16	17	18	19
Ever had intercourse	9	16	23	30	42	59	71	82
Never had intercourse	91	84	77	70	58	41	29	18

Sources: Women and men: AGI tabulations of data from the 1990 Youth Risk Behavior Survey. **Women:** AGI tabulations of data from the 1988 National Survey of Family Growth. **Men:** F. L. Sonenstein, J. H. Pleck and L. C. Ku, "Sexual Activity, Condom Use and AIDS Awareness Among Adolescent Males," *Family Planning Perspectives*, **21**:152–158, 1989, Table 1, p. 153. **Total population:** F. W. Hollmann, "Estimates of the Population of the United States by Age, Sex and Race," *Current Population Reports*, Series P-25, No. 1095, 1993, Table 1, p. 10.

Note: The National Survey of Family Growth (NSFG) and the NSAM (National Survey of Adolescent Males) do not survey youth under age 15. Estimates of age at first intercourse for 12–14-year-olds are based on data from the Youth Risk Behavior Survey (YRBS). Because the YRBS reports higher levels of sexual activity than the other two surveys, YRBS estimates were deflated on the basis of the ratio of YRBS to NSFG (or to NSAM for males) figures on proportions of 18-year-olds who have had intercourse.

FIGURE 9

♦ Young people today typically begin sexual intercourse roughly eight years before marriage—about 10 years for young men and seven years for young women.[63]

♦ The gap between first intercourse and marriage is especially long for black adolescents—about 12 years for women and 19 years for men—because they usually initiate sex relatively early and marry late.[64] Indeed, for blacks, the question is often whether they will ever marry, rather than when they will do so.[65]

SEX IN TEENAGE YEARS INCREASINGLY COMMON

Over the past three decades, growing proportions of women and men have become sexually active in their teens. Today, 56% of women and 73% of men have had intercourse before their 18th birthday.

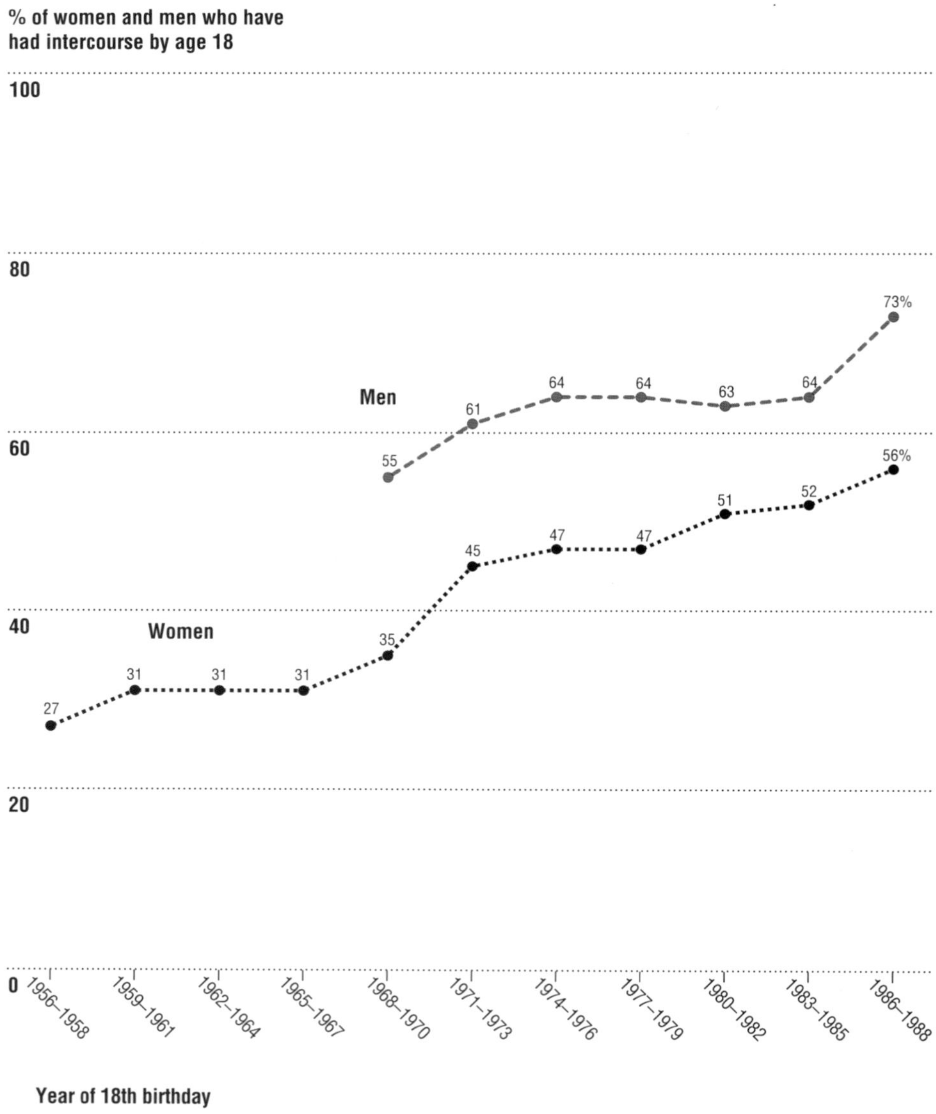

% of women and men who have had intercourse by age 18

Year of 18th birthday

Sources: Women: Adapted by AGI from tabulations by S. L. Hofferth of data from the 1982 National Survey of Family Growth; AGI tabulations of data from the 1988 National Survey of Family Growth. **Men:** Adapted by AGI from tabulations by K. Tanfer of data from the 1991 National Survey of Men.

Note: When data for the same birth cohorts were available in both the 1982 and the 1988 National Surveys of Family Growth, the percentage of women who had had sex by age 18 was calculated by taking the average of the two figures.

FIGURE 10

The trends toward increasing and earlier levels of nonmarital intercourse among young women have occurred almost entirely among whites, in part because sexual activity was already more common, and marriage less common, among black women[66] (Figure 14, page 25).

♦ The likelihood that a white teenage woman would have intercourse outside marriage more than doubled between the late 1950s and mid-1980s; as a result, 95% of sexually experienced white teenagers in the later period had been unmarried at first intercourse, compared with fewer than 60% in the late 1950s.

♦ By comparison, a black woman's likelihood increased less than 10%.

Although the level of sexual intercourse varies widely among women between the ages of 15 and 19, among this age-group as a whole, there are more similarities than differences in levels of sexual activity by race, income, religion and place of residence[67] (Figure 15, page 26).

The same trend is evident among young men, although the change has been less dramatic.[68]

♦ The proportion of never-married white men aged 17–19 living in metropolitan areas who had had sex rose from 65% in 1979 to 73% in 1988.

♦ Among never-married, metropolitan blacks, the proportion increased from 71% to 88% during that period.

Characteristics of Teenagers Who Have Sex

Age is the most important factor in determining whether a teenager is sexually experienced: The older an adolescent is, the more likely he or she is to have had sex. Various factors influence whether young teenagers have sex.[69]

♦ Among young men, the pace and timing of pubertal development is the key factor.

♦ Among white women, the influence of parents and friends is especially important; living with both parents is associated with a decrease in the likelihood of having sex at an early age, while having girlfriends or boyfriends who have already had intercourse increases the chances.

♦ Among young black women, pubertal development is the strongest predictor of having intercourse at an early age.

Sex is more common among adolescent men than women, and more likely among black teenagers than among white or Hispanic youth.

♦ At each age between 12 and 19, the proportion of young men who report having had sex roughly equals that among women who are one year older. To some degree, however, these differences may reflect that men tend to overreport sexual behaviors out of a sense that they are expected to have sex, and women tend to underreport them.[70]

♦ Half of young black men say they have had sex by age 15, but Hispanic and white men do not report this level of sexual activity until they are nearly 17.

♦ Half of black women report having had intercourse by age 16.5—a year sooner than white and Hispanic women.[71]

Family income is also a factor: Poor and low-income teenagers are more likely than adolescents from higher income families to be sexually experienced, although the difference is not as great as those among racial and ethnic groups.[72]

♦ Half of young men from families with incomes below $20,000 report having had sex by age 16, about six months sooner than higher income males.

♦ Half of young women who are poor or low-income say they have had sex by age 17, about four months sooner than higher income adolescent women.

Adolescents who engage in other high-risk behavior, such as drinking and drug use, may also be more likely than others to be sexually experienced. In the early teenage years, at least, those who frequently smoke, drink and use drugs are more likely than others to have sex[73] (Figure 16, page 27).

The Character of Teenage Sex

Little information exists about sexual behaviors other than intercourse, among adults as well as adolescents, in part because of political opposition to government support for gathering such data.[74] Information that is available, however, suggests that patterns of sexual intercourse among young people, who are almost all unmarried, differ from those

While the likelihood of having intercourse increases steadily with age, nearly 20% of adolescents do not have sex at all during their teenage years.

among older adults, who are much more likely to be married.

Coercion, Pressure and Choice. For some young people, having sex is not a voluntary choice. The youngest teenagers are especially vulnerable to coercive sex.

♦ Some 74% of women who had intercourse before age 14 and 60% of those who had sex before age 15 report having had sex involuntarily[75] (Figure 17, page 28).

♦ In 1987, 7% of sexually experienced young people aged 18–22 reported that they had been forced to have sex against their will at least once.[76]

Such information challenges society's expectation that young people, especially women, can always take responsibility for using contraceptives to prevent unintended pregnancy and sexually transmitted infections. It also raises concerns about

MORE TEENAGE MEN ARE HAVING SEX...

Higher proportions of teenage men had had sex
in the late 1980s than in the early 1970s.

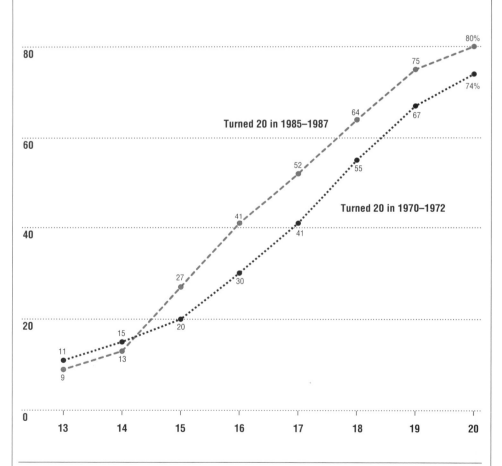

% of men who have had intercourse by each age

Turned 20 in 1985–1987

Turned 20 in 1970–1972

Source: Adapted by AGI from tabulations by K. Tanfer of data from the 1991 Survey of Men.

Note: Data are based on men aged 21–23 and 36–38 in 1988.

FIGURE 11

the impact of forced intercourse on adolescents' future sexual relationships and teenagers' ability to protect themselves from STDs and pregnancy. Studies suggest, for example, that often, people who have been sexually abused have difficulty practicing protective behaviors.[77]

Teenagers who are not forced outright may nonetheless be pressured by a partner or a friend into having sex. Some 25% of 13–17-year-olds in 1988 said they had felt pressured by their peers to have sex; young women were somewhat more likely than young men to have felt such pressure.[78] On the positive side, it appears that most teenagers do not feel pressure to have sex before they are ready.

"Serial Monogamy." Patterns of sexual relationships are often quite different for married and unmarried people, regard-

---

...AND MORE TEENAGE WOMEN ARE HAVING SEX, TOO.

Higher proportions of young women had had sex
in the late 1980s than in the late 1950s.

% of women who have had intercourse by each age

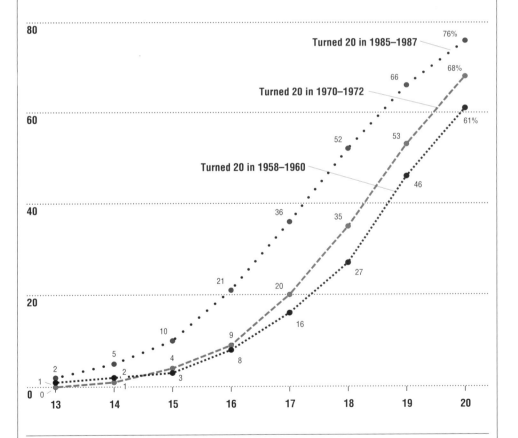

Sources: Turned 20 in 1958–1960: Adapted by AGI from tabulations by S. L. Hofferth of data from the 1982 National Survey of Family Growth. **Turned 20 in 1970–1972:** Adapted by AGI from tabulations by S. L. Hofferth of data from the 1982 National Survey of Family Growth; AGI tabulations of data from the 1988 National Survey of Family Growth. **Turned 20 in 1985–1987:** AGI tabulations of data from the 1988 National Survey of Family Growth.

Note: Data are based on women aged 30–32 and 42–44 in 1982, and aged 21–23 and 36–38 in 1988.

FIGURE 12

less of their age. Since most teenagers who have had intercourse are not married, their behavior is more similar to that of older unmarried individuals than to that of married couples.

Because of concerns about STDs, especially HIV, health officials and medical professionals advise sexually active individuals to have only one partner—

that is, to be in a mutually monogamous relationship. Unmarried people, young and old alike, often translate this advice into "serial monogamy"; in other words, they remain faithful to their partner until the relationship breaks up, but then move to another relationship, thereby increasing their risk of acquiring an STD.

Adolescent women who are sexually experienced are no more likely than older unmarried women to have more than one partner in a given period; about 10% of single, noncohabiting women aged 15–19 and in their 20s have two or more partners in a three-month period.[79]

Furthermore, most teenagers move slowly from one sexual partner to another.[80]

♦ Half of sexually experienced young women wait almost 18 months between the time they first have intercourse and the time they have a second sexual partner; for another one-quarter, the gap is almost two years.

♦ Women who begin sexual activity at a young age move more quickly than others to a second partner.

♦ Among sexually experienced women aged 15–17, 55% have had two or more partners; 13% have had sex with at least six men.

♦ By their early 20s, 71% of women who are sexually experienced have had more than one partner, and 21% have had six or more partners.

♦ On average, young men report having had more sexual partners since first intercourse than young women of similar ages, in part because they have been having sex longer.[81]

Sporadic Sex. Unmarried, sexually active men and women, including teenagers, are more likely than married people to have sex sporadically.[82]

♦ Sexually experienced, never-married women aged 15–19 have intercourse, on average, during eight out of 12 months, but a quarter have intercourse in fewer than six months out of a year; about a third of those surveyed in 1988 had not had sex in the previous month.

♦ Unmarried teenagers have intercourse less frequently than older single people (Figure 18, page 29).

MUCH LATER MARRIAGE

Following a big drop after World War II, age at first marriage has risen sharply, to 24 for women and 26 for men.

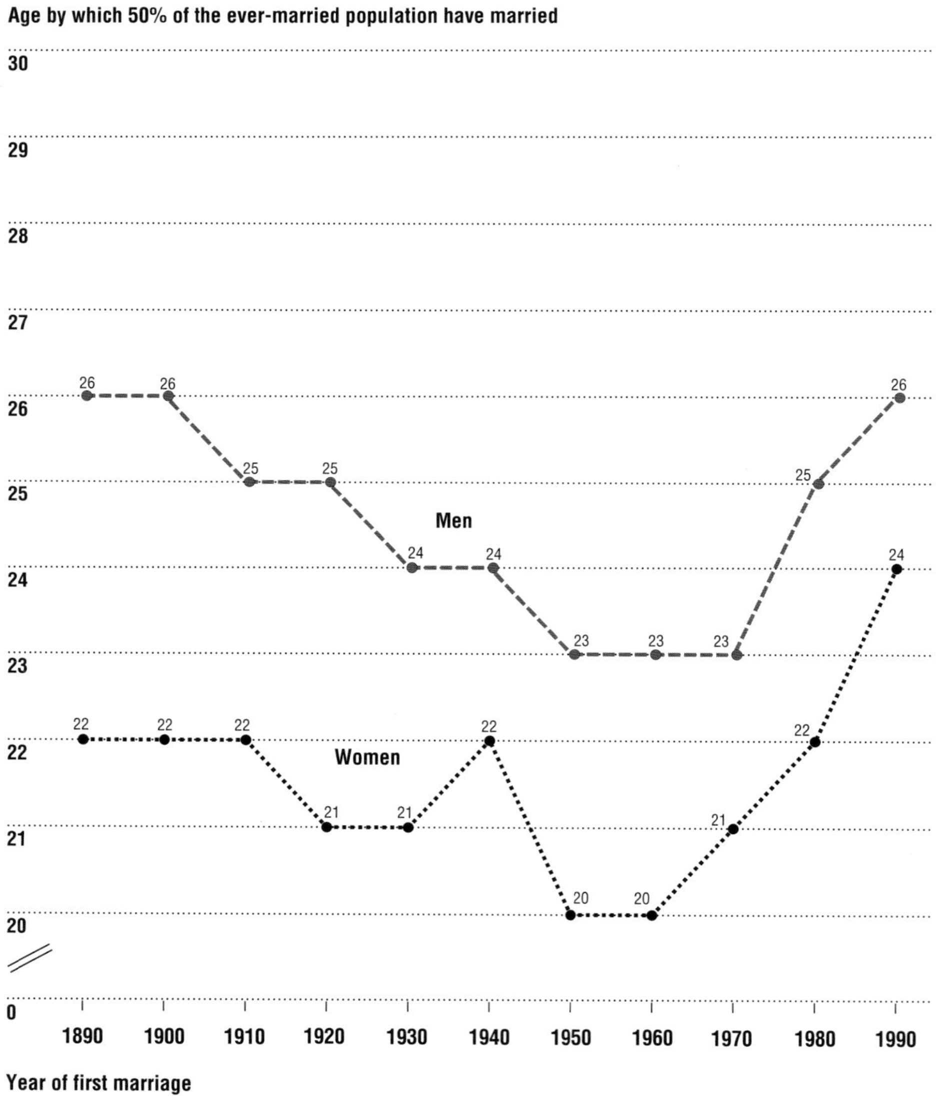

Age by which 50% of the ever-married population have married

Year of first marriage

Source: U.S. Bureau of the Census, "Marital Status and Living Arrangements, 1990," *Current Population Reports*, Series P-20, No. 450, 1991, Table A, p. 1.

Note: Data in Figure 13 for 1990 are slightly different from those in Figure 1 for 1988 both because of the difference in time and because data in Figure 13 are for the ever-married only.

FIGURE 13

♦ The small number of teenagers who are married or cohabiting, on the other hand, have intercourse more frequently than older couples who are living together.[83]

◆◆◆◆

Most young people begin to have sex in their middle or late teens, many years before they are married. The increase in nonmarital intercourse has been most dramatic among young white women. Although sex is more common among teenagers and generally begins at earlier ages than was the case several decades ago, sexually experienced adolescents tend to have intercourse less frequently than older unmarried men and women. This tendency to have sex sporadically can affect teenagers' efforts to prevent STDs and unintended pregnancy by making them unprepared to use contraceptives when they do have intercourse or unwilling to use effective methods that provide protection over a long period of time, such as the pill.

MORE SEX NOW BEFORE MARRIAGE

First intercourse among all teenagers is almost twice as likely to occur before marriage as it was 30 years ago. The change is particularly striking among whites.

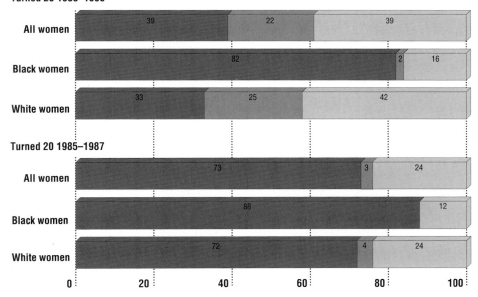

Turned 20 1958–1960

All women: 39 | 22 | 39
Black women: 82 | 2 | 16
White women: 33 | 25 | 42

Turned 20 1985–1987

All women: 73 | 3 | 24
Black women: 88 | 12
White women: 72 | 4 | 24

% of women who had had intercourse before age 20

- Before marriage
- After marriage
- No intercourse by age 20

Sources: Adapted by AGI from tabulations by S. L. Hofferth of data from the 1982 National Survey of Family Growth; AGI tabulations of data from the 1988 National Survey of Family Growth; S. L. Hofferth, J. R. Kahn and W. Baldwin, "Premarital Sexual Activity Among U.S. Teenage Women over the Past Three Decades," *Family Planning Perspectives*, **19**:46–53, 1987, Table 3, p. 49.

Note: In this figure, the terms "black" and "white" refer to race; Hispanics are categorized by race, not ethnicity.

FIGURE 14

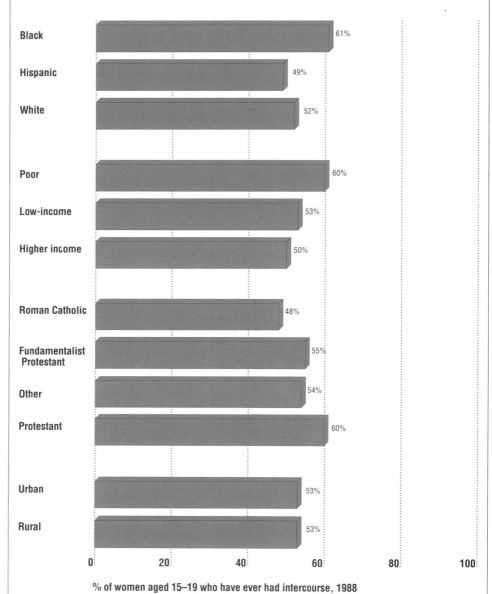

WOMEN NOW MORE SIMILAR THAN DIFFERENT

About half of women aged 15–19 have had intercourse,
regardless of race, income, religion or location.

Black — 61%
Hispanic — 49%
White — 52%

Poor — 60%
Low-income — 53%
Higher income — 50%

Roman Catholic — 48%
Fundamentalist Protestant — 55%
Other — 54%
Protestant — 60%

Urban — 53%
Rural — 53%

0   20   40   60   80   100

% of women aged 15–19 who have ever had intercourse, 1988

Sources: J. D. Forrest and S. Singh, "The Sexual and
Reproductive Behavior of American Women, 1982–1988,"
Family Planning Perspectives, **22**:206–214, 1990, Table 4,
p. 208; AGI tabulations of data from the 1988 National
Survey of Family Growth.

FIGURE 15

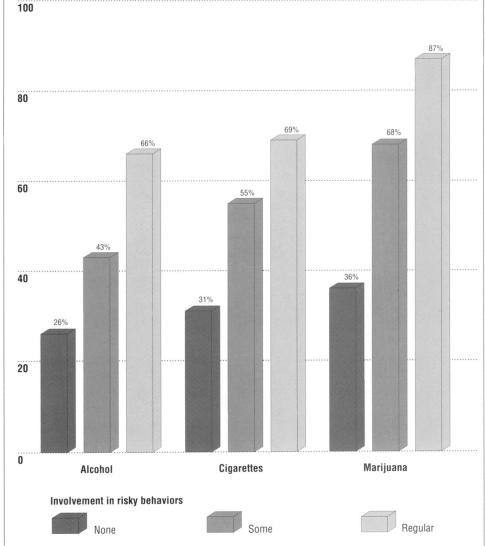

RISK-TAKING AND EARLY SEX

The more involved 14–15-year-olds are in drinking or smoking, the more likely they are to have had intercourse.

% of 14–15-year-olds who
have had intercourse, 1990

Alcohol

Cigarettes

Marijuana

Involvement in risky behaviors

None

Some

Regular

The likelihood that a white teenage woman would have intercourse outside marriage more than doubled between the late 1950s and mid-1980s.

Source: AGI tabulations of data from the 1990 Youth Risk Behavior Survey.

Notes: Alcohol and marijuana: "Regular" involvement is defined as use on three or more occasions in the last 30 days.

"Some" involvement is defined as use on one or two occasions in the last 30 days. **Cigarettes:** "Regular" involvement is defined as smoking six times or more in the past 30 days. "Some" involvement is defined as smoking cigarettes 1–5 times in the past 30 days.

FIGURE 16

Some 74% of women who had intercourse before age 14 and 60% of those who had sex before age 15 report having had sex involuntarily.

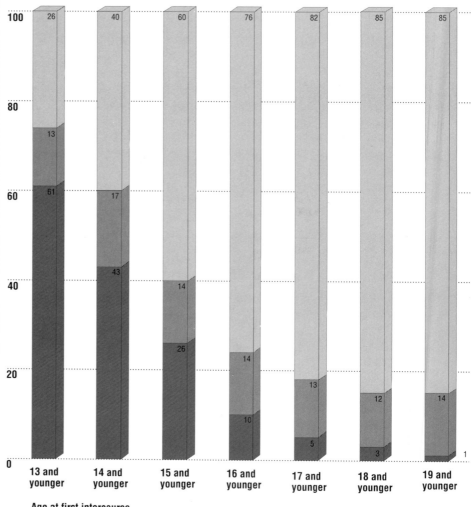

FORCED SEX

The younger a sexually experienced teenager is,
the more likely she is to have had involuntary sex.

% of women aged 19 and younger who have had intercourse

26	40	60	76	82	85	85
13	17	14	14	13	12	14
61	43	26	10	5	3	1

13 and younger / 14 and younger / 15 and younger / 16 and younger / 17 and younger / 18 and younger / 19 and younger

Age at first intercourse

 Involuntary intercourse only

 Both voluntary and involuntary intercourse

 Voluntary intercourse only

Source: Adapted by AGI from tabulations by K. A. Moore, C. W. Nord and J. L. Peterson of data from the 1987 National Survey of Children. See K. A. Moore, C. W. Nord and J. L. Peterson, "Nonvoluntary Sexual Activity Among Adolescents," *Family Planning Perspectives,* **21**:110–114, 1989, Table 2, p. 111.

Note: Those who answered affirmatively to the question "Was there ever a time when you were forced to have sex against your will, or were raped?" were classified as having had involuntary intercourse.

FIGURE 17

FREQUENCY OF INTERCOURSE

Unmarried teenagers have sex less often than do single women in their early 20s.

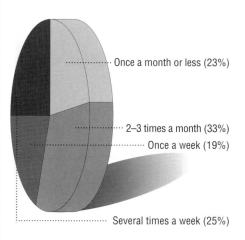

Once a month or less (23%)

2–3 times a month (33%)
Once a week (19%)

Several times a week (25%)

**Unmarried sexually experienced women
aged 15–19, 1988: 4,226,000**

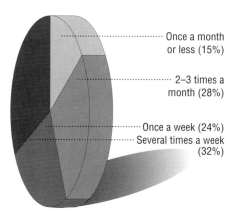

Once a month
or less (15%)

2–3 times a
month (28%)

Once a week (24%)
Several times a week
(32%)

**Unmarried sexually experienced women
aged 20–24, 1988: 4,246,000**

Source: AGI tabulations of data from the 1988 National Survey of Family Growth.

Note: Calculations show frequency of intercourse within three months prior to survey among unmarried sexually experienced women not cohabiting.

FIGURE 18

Risks and Prevention of Unintended Pregnancy and STDs

A fertile woman has about a 3% chance of becoming pregnant in a single act of unprotected intercourse, although the risk ranges from virtually zero to 30%, depending on when during the menstrual cycle intercourse occurs.[84] Within a year, however, a sexually active teenager who does not use a contraceptive has a 90% chance of becoming pregnant[85] (Figure 19, page 30).

Other things being equal, teenagers and women in their early 20s theoretically have a higher risk of pregnancy than older women, because the ability to conceive declines slowly after the mid-20s.[86] However, pregnancy levels may be relatively low in the first few years after puberty, before regular ovulation and sperm production are established.[87] In addition, since unmarried sexually active teenagers generally have less-frequent intercourse than older unmarried individuals, they may experience lower pregnancy rates.

The chance of acquiring a sexually transmitted infection may be substantially greater than the risk of becoming pregnant, although the likelihood varies considerably, depending on one's sex, on whether one's partner has an STD and on what the disease is. Women are at greater risk of acquiring an STD than men, because anatomical differences make many of these diseases more easily transmissible to women.[88]

♦ In a single act of unprotected intercourse with an infected partner, for example, a woman is twice as likely as a man to acquire gonorrhea or chlamydia (Figure 20, page 31), as well as hepatitis B (not shown).

♦ Some STDs are more easily transmissible than others, however. For example, in a single act of unprotected intercourse with an infected partner, a woman has a 1% risk of acquiring HIV, a 30% risk of getting genital herpes and a 50% chance of contracting gonorrhea; a man's risk of infection ranges from 1% for HIV to 30% for genital herpes.

The more partners an individual has, the higher the risk of being exposed to a sexually transmitted infection.

♦ Overall, younger women are more likely than older women to have more than one partner in a three-month period, because most are unmarried[89] (Figure 21, page 32).

♦ Many teenagers, as well as adults, are indirectly exposed to more than one sexual partner each year because their partner has had sex with someone else.[90]

RISK OF PREGNANCY

A sexually active teenage woman using no contraceptive over the course of a year has a 90% chance of becoming pregnant.

Estimated % of women becoming pregnant in one year of intercourse using no contraceptive method

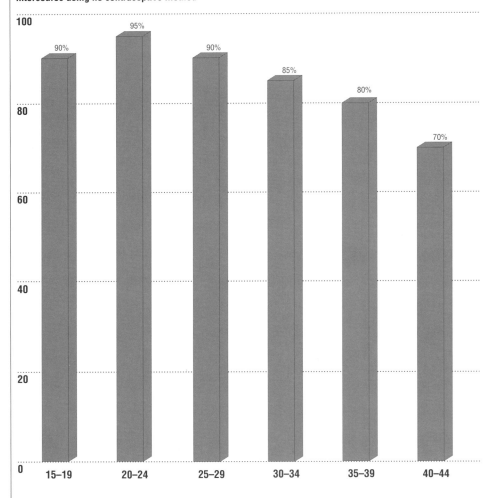

Source: S. Harlap, K. Kost and J. D. Forrest, *Preventing Pregnancy, Protecting Health: A New Look at Birth Control*

Choices in the United States, AGI, New York, 1991, Table 8.2, p. 121.

FIGURE 19

In addition, adolescent women may be biologically more susceptible to sexually transmitted infections than older women. Young women may have a higher risk of cervical infections because their cervix has not completely undergone age-related developmental changes.[91] In addition, they have fewer protective STD antibodies.[92]

Correct and consistent use of a latex condom[93] at each act of intercourse markedly reduces the risk of acquiring an STD, including HIV.[94] Even imperfect use[95] reduces the risk by about 50%.[96] By contrast, in a year of regular intercourse with a man infected with gonorrhea, an estimated 90% of women would become infected if they used no method, a hormonal method, periodic abstinence or the IUD; an estimated 60–70% would become infected if they used the diaphragm or spermicide alone.[97]

The Difficulties of Prevention

Although contraceptives can prevent pregnancy and STDs, they can be complicated to use, and some may seem inappropriate to teenagers who have sex sporadically. In addition, contraceptives can be difficult or expensive for adolescents to obtain.

Planning. All contraceptive methods other than withdrawal require planning, either to obtain supplies or to give the method time to take effect. (It is generally recommended, for example, that for the first several days after a woman begins to use the pill, she and her partner also use a second method.) Planning can be difficult, especially in the early stages of a relationship, when it may not be clear whether or when intercourse might occur. In addition, ambivalence about sex and a romantic desire to be "swept away" can impede the willingness of people who are not in a long-standing relationship to be prepared "just in case."[98]

Some methods, such as the male condom, the female condom and spermicides, are available without a prescription. Their relative accessibility and low cost make it feasible to keep them on hand in case they are needed. (This may be problematic for teenagers who do not want their parents to know they have contraceptives—and therefore, presumably, are having sex.) On the other hand, use of any of these methods is usually apparent to one's partner and may even require the partner's

cooperation. The necessary communication and agreement between partners may be awkward to achieve in a new relationship, and may be especially difficult for teenage women, whose partners often are considerably older.[99] (It may also be difficult to introduce or continue using condoms in long-standing relationships.[100])

Other methods—hormonal methods, such as the pill, the contraceptive implant or the injectable contraceptive; and the

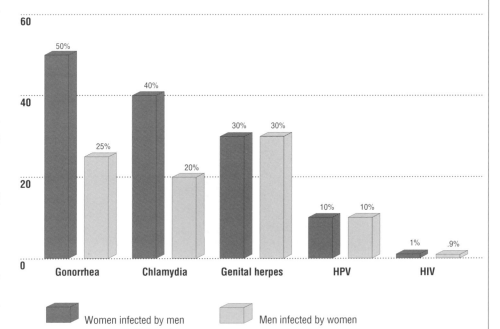

STD RISK, BY GENDER

Women are at least as likely as men to acquire certain STDs during a single act of unprotected intercourse with an infected partner.

Estimated % risk of acquiring an STD in one act of unprotected intercourse with an infected partner, all ages

Source: S. Harlap, K. Kost and J. D. Forrest, *Preventing Pregnancy, Protecting Health: A New Look at Birth Control Choices in the United States,* AGI, New York, 1991, Figure 6.4, p. 43.

Notes: HPV is human papillomavirus. **HIV** is human immunodeficiency virus.

FIGURE 20

diaphragm—require a medical visit prior to use and either a prescription or insertion or injection by a clinician. (IUDs are seldom offered to young women because of the possible risks of infection leading to infertility.) A woman can use any of these methods, with the possible exception of the diaphragm, without her partner's knowledge; however, the continuous protection against pregnancy provided by these

methods, as well as by periodic abstinence (which requires ongoing monitoring of the time of ovulation), may seem unnecessary to women who do not have sex regularly.[101]

In addition, hormonal methods and periodic abstinence offer no protection against STDs, although hormonal methods do lower a woman's risk of developing an upper genital tract infection if she contracts certain diseases.[102] Thus, a woman relying on one of these methods must also use a barrier method—preferably, the male condom—to protect herself or her partner against STDs as well as pregnancy.

Obtaining Methods. Acquiring the services and supplies needed to prevent pregnancy or STDs can be difficult or even forbidding for teenagers.

♦ Many people are embarrassed to buy condoms.[103]

♦ Clinicians often do not initiate discussion about contraception and STDs with adolescents, who may be too timid or embarrassed to raise such subjects themselves.[104]

♦ Young women seeking the pill and other prescription methods may be embarrassed to have a pelvic examination[105] or may not know how to locate a physician on their own, since a pediatrician is probably the only doctor many teenagers have seen on a regular basis.

♦ More than a quarter of private doctors who write pill prescriptions will not do so for a minor without her parent's consent[106]—a restriction that inhibits some young people from seeking sensitive health care.[107]

Services at family planning clinics, community health centers and other publicly supported clinics are the easiest for teenagers to obtain. Family planning clinics, for example, rarely require parental consent, although clinicians strongly urge young women, especially very young teenagers, to talk with their parents.[108] In addition, many clinics provide services and pills to young women without charge; when they do charge, clinics' fees are generally lower than those of private practitioners,[109] who typically charge $55–$89 for a new patient visit, not including laboratory fees.[110] Clinics are also more likely than private doctors to have evening and weekend hours, and to see patients without an appointment. In addition, they are

MULTIPLE PARTNERS

Younger women are more likely than older women to have more than one sexual partner in a short time period because most younger women are unmarried. Among the unmarried only, age makes little difference in the proportions with multiple sexual partners.

% of women sexually active in the last three months who had more than one sexual partner in that time period, 1988

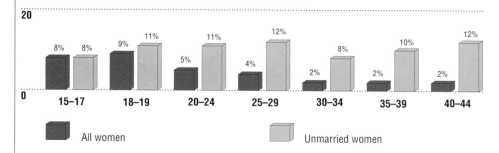

	15–17	18–19	20–24	25–29	30–34	35–39	40–44
All women	8%	9%	5%	4%	2%	2%	2%
Unmarried women	8%	11%	11%	12%	8%	10%	12%

■ All women   ▢ Unmarried women

Sources: All women: K. Kost and J. D. Forrest, "American Women's Sexual Behavior and Exposure to Risk of Sexually Transmitted Diseases," *Family Planning Perspectives,* 24:244–254, 1992, Table 3, p. 248. **Unmarried women:** AGI tabulations of data from the 1988 National Survey of Family Growth.
Note: Unmarried women exclude those who are currently married and those who are cohabiting.

FIGURE 21

substantially more likely to serve a woman who cannot pay.[111] Between 1980 and 1992, however, funding for the Title X family planning program, which provides crucial support for clinics, declined 72% (adjusted for inflation).[112] As a consequence, some clinics have been forced to charge higher fees, cut back their hours of operation or reduce education and outreach efforts—changes that make services less accessible to teenagers.[113]

In recent years, in an effort to make services more accessible to young people, a number of school-based and school-linked clinics have opened, and condom distribution programs have been implemented in some schools. Only a third of these clinics dispense contraceptives on site,[114] however, and only a handful of schools have established condom distribution programs.[115]

Contraceptive Use Among Sexually Experienced Teenagers

Despite the barriers, most sexually experienced teenagers use contraceptives.

♦ Contraceptive use among teenagers, particularly condom use, increased considerably between 1982 and 1988.[116]

♦ Many young people use two methods—one to protect themselves or their partners against pregnancy and another to prevent STD transmission (although it is not clear from the data available how many use both methods simultaneously). A quarter of the 1.7 million teenagers who use the pill, for example, also use condoms. Of men aged 15–19 who use condoms, a quarter use them in combination with a female method.[117]

Use at First Intercourse. Two-thirds of adolescents use some method of contraception—usually the male condom—the first time they have sexual intercourse.[118]

♦ The older a teenager is at first intercourse, the more likely she or he is to use a contraceptive.[119]

♦ Whites are substantially more likely than blacks or Hispanics, and higher income teenagers are more likely than poor or low-income adolescents, to use a method the first time they have sex.[120]

♦ The prevalence of condom use at first intercourse among women aged 15–19 jumped from 23% to 48% between 1982

and 1988; the increase occurred among young women of all races, ethnic groups and income levels[121] (Figure 22, page 33).

♦ Even so, white and higher income teenagers are more likely than others to use condoms at first intercourse.[122]

GETTING BETTER AT PRECAUTIONS

Teenage women's contraceptive use at first intercourse rose from 48% in 1982 to 65% in 1988. Condom use doubled.

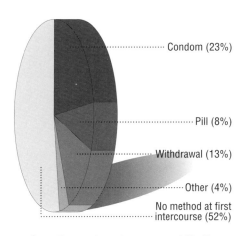

Condom (23%)

Pill (8%)

Withdrawal (13%)

Other (4%)

No method at first intercourse (52%)

Sexually experienced women aged 15–19 at interview, 1982: 4,484,000

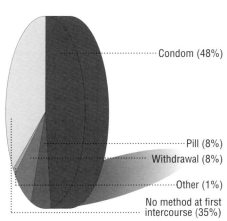

Condom (48%)

Pill (8%)

Withdrawal (8%)

Other (1%)

No method at first intercourse (35%)

Sexually experienced women aged 15–19 at interview, 1988: 4,883,000

Source: J. D. Forrest and S. Singh, "The Sexual and Reproductive Behavior of American Women, 1982–1988," *Family Planning Perspectives*, **22**:206–214, 1990, Table 5, p. 209.

FIGURE 22

DELAYS STILL COMMON

Most young women are sexually active for a substantial time before they go to a doctor or a clinic; only 40% go for medical contraceptive services within the first year after they begin intercourse.

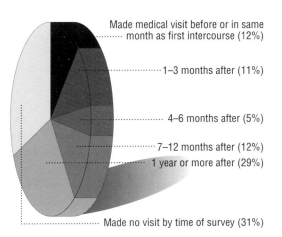

Made medical visit before or in same month as first intercourse (12%)

1–3 months after (11%)

4–6 months after (5%)

7–12 months after (12%)

1 year or more after (29%)

Made no visit by time of survey (31%)

Sexually experienced women aged 15–19 who have been sexually active for at least a year, 1988: 3,650,000

Source: AGI tabulations of data from the 1988 National Survey of Family Growth.

FIGURE 23

Delay in Seeking Medical Services.
It is important for sexually experienced
teenagers, especially young women, to
visit a clinic or doctor not only to obtain
more effective contraceptives, but also to
undergo periodic STD screening and, if
necessary, treatment. Most sexually
experienced teenagers who use birth control, however, rely on over-the-counter
methods, such as the condom, for a considerable period before they consult a
medical professional.[123]

◆ Only 40% of sexually experienced teenage women visit a doctor or clinic for con-

traceptives within 12 months of beginning
intercourse (Figure 23, page 33).

◆ Black teenagers and adolescents from
poor families make a family planning visit
sooner than whites or Hispanics and
teenagers from higher income families.[124]

◆ Women who are older when they first
have intercourse are more likely than
younger teenagers to make a family planning visit soon after they first have sex
(although they are no more likely to go to
a clinic or doctor for contraceptives before
the month in which they first have sex).[125]

Two-thirds of all adolescent women,
and even higher proportions of those who
are poor or who begin sex at an early age,
first seek medical contraceptive services
from a family planning clinic.[126]

◆ Clinics continue to be the most common
source of medical services well after the
first visit.

◆ In 1988, a clinic was the most recent
source of services for almost two-thirds of
women aged 15–19, including three-quarters of those who were poor.

Current Contraceptive Use. At any giv-
en time, three-quarters of adolescent
women who have had sex are at risk of
unintended pregnancy.[127] Most at-risk
teenagers use contraceptives.[128]

◆ Some 72% of 15–17-year-old women at
risk and 84% of 18–19-year-olds use some
method of contraception, as do 88% of
women aged 20–24 (Figure 24, page 34).

◆ In general, pill use increases and condom use declines with age; however, the
reverse is true for Hispanic women.

◆ Black and Hispanic teenagers are less
likely than white adolescents to use some
method of contraception, although the difference between blacks and whites is
small. Blacks, however, are more likely
than whites to use the pill.

◆ Higher income teenagers are much more
likely than low-income teenagers and
somewhat more likely than poor adolescents to use contraceptives. Poor women,
however, are slightly more likely than their
more advantaged peers to use the pill.

◆ Differences in pill use by race and ethnicity and by income may reflect, at least in
part, poor and black teenagers' tendency to
visit a clinic or doctor for contraceptives rel-

TRYING TO AVOID PREGNANCY

On an ongoing basis, the majority of sexually experienced adolescent women
and their partners use a contraceptive, primarily the condom or the pill.

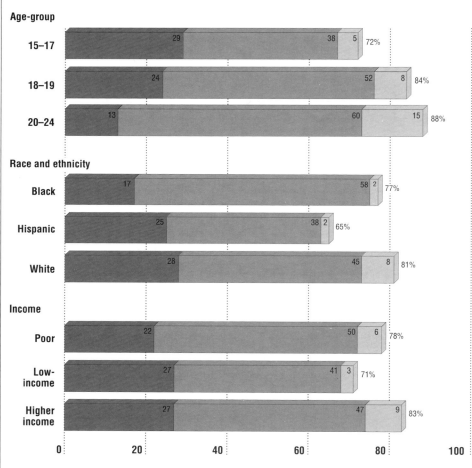

% of women aged 15–19 at risk of unintended pregnancy who are using a contraceptive, 1988

Source: AGI tabulations of data from the 1988 National
Survey of Family Growth.

Note: Data on age-groups only include 20–24-year-olds.

FIGURE 24

atively soon after they begin intercourse. **Less Than Perfect Use.** Successful use of most reversible contraceptive methods requires both motivation and a constancy of attention and action that is difficult for married adults, let alone teenagers and others who are not in stable, long-term relationships, to maintain.[129]

♦ Among all women who rely on condoms, only eight in 10 used one at last intercourse; only two in 10 of those who rely on condoms solely for protection against STDs used one the last time they had sex.

♦ Teenage women who use condoms to prevent an unintended pregnancy are as likely to have used one at last intercourse as are older women with similar numbers of partners, income and race or ethnicity.

Successful use of condoms and pills, as well as of other reversible methods, generally requires adherence to certain steps. Most women who use condoms or the pill do not follow all of these steps; teenage women do about as well as older women in this regard[130] (Figures 25 and 26, pages 35 and 36).

Teenagers' Success in Avoiding Pregnancy

Even though their use is not always perfect, a large majority of never-married adolescents who use contraceptives succeed in avoiding unintended pregnancy. Indeed, they do at least as well as older women[131] (Figure 27, page 37).

♦ Never-married teenagers are slightly more successful than never-married women aged 20–24 in preventing an accidental pregnancy in the first 12 months of pill or condom use.

♦ Teenagers are about as likely to prevent an unintended pregnancy as are never-married women aged 25–29 using the same contraceptives.

♦ The relatively low rate of unintended pregnancies among never-married adolescents using the pill and condoms may reflect, in part, that they have intercourse less frequently than older never-married women.

At all ages, women who are poor or low-income have more difficulty than higher income women in using contraceptives effectively: Unintended pregnancy rates among pill and condom users who are poor or low-income are about twice those among higher income women.[132]

In contrast to the fairly small differences in unintended pregnancy rates

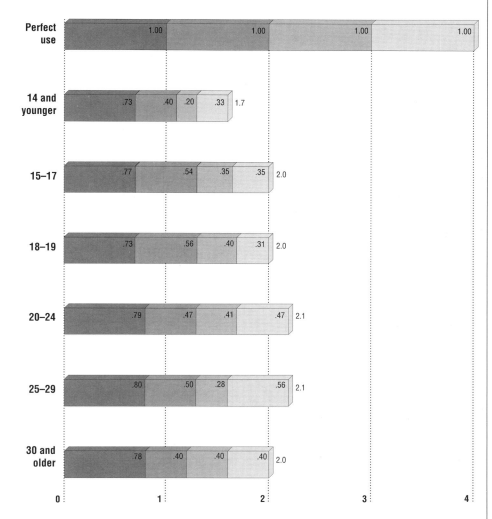

CONDOM USE NEEDS IMPROVEMENT AT ALL AGES.

Teenagers do almost as well as older women in trying to follow the criteria for perfect condom use.

Average number and type of criteria met for good condom use out of total of four

Put condom on prior to penetration

Hold condom in place during withdrawal

Withdraw while penis is still erect

Use a condom during every act of intercourse

Source: Tabulations by D. Oakley of data from the University of Michigan longitudinal survey of initial clients at three family planning clinics near Detroit, Feb. 1987–Apr. 1989.

Note: Condoms were the main contraceptive method used for any study month, and women were sexually active at least one of those months.

FIGURE 25

among never-married women of various ages, there are strong age differences among reversible contraceptive users who

have ever been married. Rates are about twice as high for ever-married teenage users as they are for never-married adolescent women, while pregnancy rates for users aged 20–24 do not vary substantially by marital status. In fact, ever-married adolescents have the highest unintended pregnancy rates, regardless of whether they use the pill or the condom and regardless of their poverty status.[133] The higher rates among younger married users may reflect weaker motivation to delay pregnancy, greater frequency of intercourse, higher fertility or selection of women more likely to have accidental pregnancies into earlier marriage.

◆◆◆◆

Contraceptives can significantly reduce the risk of becoming pregnant or of acquiring an STD—in some cases, virtually to zero. Although contraceptives can be difficult for teenagers to obtain and to use, most sexually experienced adolescents try to behave responsibly by protecting themselves and their partners from disease and unintended pregnancy. In general, teenagers use contraceptives as effectively as, or even better than, unmarried adults. For adolescents who are not effective users or who do not use a method, however, the consequences can be serious.

PILL USE COULD IMPROVE, TOO.

Teenagers do almost as well as older women in trying to follow the criteria for perfect pill use.

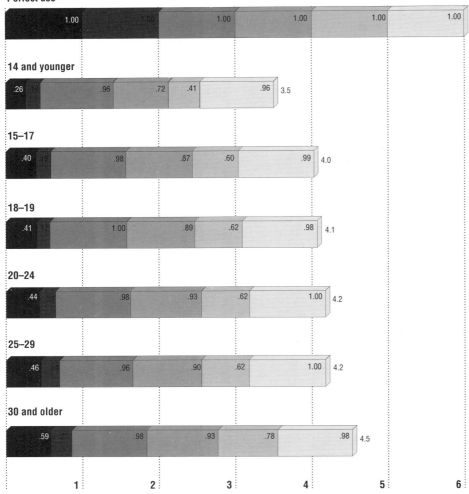

Average number and type of criteria met for good pill use out of total of six

- Take a pill every day
- Take a pill at same time every day
- Take pills in same order
- Take all pills
- Use a backup method if forget pill
- Take only own pills

Source: Tabulations by D. Oakley of data from University of Michigan longitudinal survey of initial clients at three family planning clinics near Detroit, Feb. 1987–Apr. 1989. See D. Oakley, S. Sereika and E.-L. Bogue, "Oral Contraceptive Pill Use After an Initial Visit to the Family Planning Clinic," *Family Planning Perspectives*, **23**:150–154, 1991.

Note: Oral contraceptives were the main contraceptive used for any study month, and women were sexually active at least one of those months.

FIGURE 26

TEENAGERS' SUCCESS IN PREGNANCY PREVENTION

Unmarried teenagers are less likely to have a contraceptive failure than are unmarried women in their early 20s. Overall, those who are higher income and those relying on pills have the lowest accidental pregnancy rates.

% of never-married women pregnant in first year of condom or pill use, 1984–1987

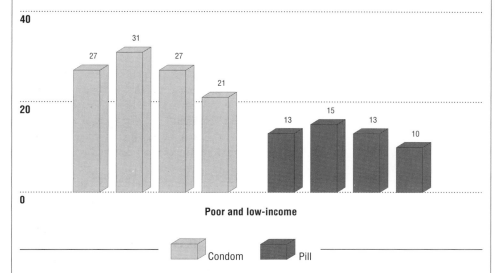

Poor and low-income

Condom   Pill

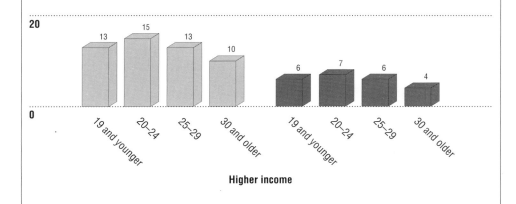

Higher income

At any given time, three-quarters of adolescent women who have had sex are at risk of unintended pregnancy. Most at-risk teenagers use contraceptives.

Source: E. F. Jones and J. D. Forrest, "Contraceptive Failure Rates Based on the 1988 NSFG," *Family Planning Perspectives,* **24**:12–19, 1992, Table 2, p. 15.

FIGURE 27

Incidence and Consequences of STDs

Every year, 3 million teenagers acquire an STD. Adolescents thus account for a quarter of the 12 million new sexually transmitted infections that occur annually in the United States[134] (Figure 28, page 38).

♦ About 25% of sexually experienced adolescents become infected each year.[135]

♦ Roughly 13% of young people between the ages of 13 and 19 contract an STD annually.[136]

The Variety of STDs

A wide variety of diseases can be transmitted through sexual intimacy. Chlamydia, trichomoniasis, gonorrhea, human papillomavirus (HPV), genital herpes, hepatitis B, syphilis and HIV are among the most common STDs. Some diseases, including chlamydia, gonorrhea, trichomoniasis and syphilis, can generally be cured quite easily if they are detected and treated early. On the other hand, viral infections—such as HPV, genital herpes, hepatitis B and HIV—cannot be cured and can be transmitted to sexual partners even years after

initial infection. Some 56 million Americans—more than one in five—are estimated to be infected with a viral STD other than HIV; 1 million are believed to have the virus that causes AIDS.[137]

Data on STD incidence and prevalence among teenagers are often incomplete or extrapolated from small clinical samples. Available information, however, suggests that some STDs are extremely common among adolescents.

♦ Between 10% and 29% of sexually experienced adolescent women tested for STDs have been found to have chlamydia.[138]

♦ Up to 15% of sexually experienced teenage women are infected with HPV; in some studies, the majority have a strain of the virus linked to cervical cancer.[139]

♦ The rate of reported cases of infectious syphilis among adolescent women has more than doubled since the mid-1980s.[140]

♦ Sexually experienced women and men aged 15–19 have higher rates of gonorrhea than any five-year age-group between 20 and 44.[141]

♦ Although the number of reported AIDS cases among teenagers is very small, about 20% of AIDS cases are diagnosed in people in their 20s, most of whom probably contracted HIV during adolescence.[142]

The Consequences of STDs

Both men and women can suffer serious health problems—such as infertility, cancer or HIV infection—as a consequence of a sexually transmitted infection (Figure 29, page 39). STDs have a disproportionate impact on women, however, because these diseases are both more easily transmitted to and more difficult to detect in women; as a result, complications of undiagnosed infections are far more common and severe in women. In addition, women can transmit an STD to their offspring during pregnancy or childbirth, sometimes with devastating consequences.[143]

Infertility. Many of the most serious problems associated with STDs result from undetected chlamydial and gonorrheal infections. If untreated, these diseases can develop into pelvic inflammatory disease (PID) in women and epididymitis

---

STD CASES, BY AGE

An estimated 3 million adolescent women and men get an STD each year, accounting for 25% of all new STDs cases annually.

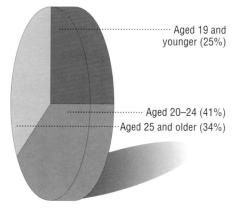

Aged 19 and younger (25%)

Aged 20–24 (41%)
Aged 25 and older (34%)

Estimated new cases of STDs, 1992: 12,000,000

Source: Centers for Disease Control and Prevention, *Division of STD/HIV Prevention, 1992 Annual Report,* Atlanta, 1993.

FIGURE 28

in men, which in turn can lead to infertility and, in women, to ectopic pregnancy. Because most sexually experienced teenage women postpone childbearing, untreated STDs are likely to have a greater impact on young women than on older women, many of whom have already begun or completed childbearing.[144]

A sexually experienced woman's risk of becoming infertile as a consequence of an upper genital tract infection (usually caused by untreated chlamydia or gonor-rhea) or of having an ectopic pregnancy (a possible result of an upper genital tract infection) is almost nonexistent if her risk of contracting an STD is low—that is, if she is in a mutually monogamous relationship with an uninfected partner. The risk of infection is substantially higher if the relationship is not mutually monogamous. In fact, being in a mutually monogamous relationship has a greater impact on reducing the risk of becoming infertile than does the choice of a contraceptive method.[145]

EFFECTS OF STDS

STDs have similar effects on women and men, including teenagers, although complications are more common in women. Chlamydia and gonorrhea can cause infertility in both women and men if not recognized and treated early.

Disease and annual incidence	Consequences for the infected person		
	Woman	Man	Fetus and newborn
CURABLE, NONVIRAL DISEASES			
Chlamydia 4 million	Pelvic inflammatory disease Ectopic pregnancy Chronic pelvic pain Infertility Increased risk of HIV if exposed	Epididymitis Infertility Increased risk of HIV if exposed	Premature delivery Pneumonia Neonatal eye infections
Trichomoniasis 3 million	Increased risk of HIV if exposed	Increased risk of HIV if exposed	Premature delivery
Gonorrhea 1.1 million	Pelvic inflammatory disease Ectopic pregnancy Infertility Infection of joints, heart valves or brain Increased risk of HIV if exposed	Infertility Infection of joints, heart valves or brain Increased risk of HIV if exposed	Blindness Meningitis Septic arthritis
Syphilis 120,000	Serious damage to many body systems Mental illness Increased risk of HIV if exposed	Serious damage to many body systems Mental illness Increased risk of HIV if exposed	Stillbirth or neonatal death Active syphilis Damage to heart, brain or eyes
Chancroid 3,500	Increased risk of HIV if exposed	Increased risk of HIV if exposed	Unknown
NONCURABLE, VIRAL DISEASES			
HPV 500,000–1 million	Cancer of cervix, vulva, vagina or anus	Cancer of penis or anus	Warts in throat that can obstruct air passages
Genital herpes 200,000–500,000	Increased risk of HIV if exposed	Increased risk of HIV if exposed	Premature delivery Serious brain damage Death
Hepatitis B 100,000–200,000	Cirrhosis Liver cancer Immune system disorders	Cirrhosis Liver cancer Immune system disorders	Liver disease Liver cancer
HIV 40,000–50,000	Immune system disorders Increased risk of other STDs	Immune system disorders Increased risk of other STDs	Immune system disorders AIDS

Sources: HIV: Centers for Disease Control and Prevention, "Projections of the Number of Persons Diagnosed with AIDS and the Number of Immunosuppressed HIV-Infected Persons, United States, 1992–1994," *Morbidity and Mortality Weekly Report*, **41:**18–19, 1992, Table 6. **All others:** P. Donovan, *Testing Positive: Sexually Transmitted Disease and the Public Health Response*, AGI, New York, 1993, pp. 10–17.

FIGURE 29

> **Sexually experienced women and men aged 15–19 have higher rates of gonorrhea than any five-year age-group between 20 and 44.**

Even those women at high risk of acquiring an STD, however, can avoid infection-induced infertility if they choose the right contraceptive method, especially if they use it consistently.

♦ On average, a woman who is in a relationship that is not mutually monogamous has a 5% risk of developing tubal infertility over a five-year period if she uses no method of contraception.[146]

♦ Barrier and spermicidal methods, especially latex condoms, offer the maximum protection. Even when used imperfectly, condoms will reduce a woman's risk of infertility to an estimated 2%; used consistently, they provide still greater protection.[147]

♦ The pill and other hormonal methods offer no protection against the risk of acquiring an STD. However, they probably lower a woman's risk of ultimately developing tubal infertility, because they reduce the chances that a lower genital tract infection will ascend into the upper genital tract, where it could develop into PID and its sequelae, and they help prevent ectopic pregnancies, which can lead to infertility.[148]

Cancer, HIV Infection. Early detection and treatment of STDs can reduce the chance that men and women will develop cancers associated with HPV and hepatitis B. In addition, a number of common infections, including syphilis, genital herpes, chlamydia, trichomoniasis and gonorrhea, increase an individual's risk of contracting HIV if exposed to that virus;[149] prompt treatment of these infections may eliminate or at least reduce that risk.

♦♦♦♦

STDs are extremely common among sexually experienced teenagers and can have serious, even life-threatening consequences. The surest means of preventing these problems is to be in a mutually monogamous relationship. Use of contraceptives, particularly latex condoms, can significantly reduce the likelihood of experiencing serious consequences, usually by lowering the risk of acquiring an STD. When infection does occur, timely treatment can be crucial to protecting one's health. STDs, of course, are not the only negative consequence of unprotected sex.

Adolescent Pregnancy

Most sexually experienced teenagers try to prevent pregnancy, and most young contraceptive users succeed in doing so. Nevertheless, 1 million adolescent women—12% of all women aged 15–19 and 21% of those who have had sexual intercourse—become pregnant every year.[150]

Pregnancy Rates: Up or Down?

Over the last two decades, adolescent pregnancy rates have gone both up and down, depending on how they are calculated (Figure 30, page 41). Reflecting the dramatic rise in the proportion of adolescent women who have had sexual intercourse during this period, the rate among all teenage women aged 15–19 increased 23% between 1972 and 1990, and is now at its highest level in nearly 20 years.[151]

Pregnancy rates among all adolescent women, however, do not present an accurate picture of pregnancy levels among teenagers, because some adolescents are not sexually experienced and therefore are not exposed to the risk of pregnancy. The more important trend, therefore, is the pregnancy rate among sexually experienced teenagers. That rate has declined 19% among 15–19-year-olds in the last two decades[152]—an encouraging indication that sexually experienced adolescents are using contraceptives more effectively than did their counterparts in the past.

Age and Race as Factors

Nearly two-thirds of teenage pregnancies occur among 18–19-year-old women.[153] The proportion of sexually experienced teenagers who become pregnant increases with age, because as they get older, adolescents generally have intercourse more frequently and are more likely to be fertile and to want to get pregnant[154] (Figure 31, page 42).

♦ Among sexually experienced teenagers, about 9% of 14-year-olds, 18% of 15–17-year-olds and 22% of 18–19-year-olds become pregnant each year.

♦ The rate for 18–19-year-olds is only slightly lower than that for 20–24-year-olds.

DECLINE AND RISE IN PREGNANCY RATES

Over the last two decades, the pregnancy rate among teenage women who have had intercourse has declined; however, since proportionately more adolescents are having intercourse, the pregnancy rate among all teenage women has increased.

Pregnancies per 1,000 women aged 15–19

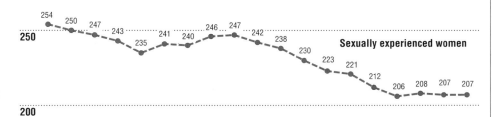

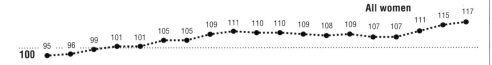

Sources: Births, 1972–1990: National Center for Health Statistics, "Advance Report of Final Natality Statistics," *Monthly Vital Statistics Report,* Vols. 23–41, Supplements, 1974–1993. **Abortions, 1973–1988:** S. K. Henshaw and J. Van Vort, eds., *Abortion Factbook, 1992 Edition: Readings, Trends, and State and Local Data to 1988,* AGI, New York, 1992, Table 1, pp. 172–173; **1972, 1989–1990:** S. K. Henshaw, "U.S. Teenage Pregnancy Statistics," AGI, New York, 1993. **Sexual experience data:** E. F. Jones et al., *Teenage Prenancy in Industrialized Countries,* Yale University Press, New Haven and London, 1986, Table 3.5, p. 47; J. D. Forrest and S. Singh, "The Sexual and Reproductive Behavior of American Women, 1982–1988," *Family Planning Perspectives,* **22**:206–214, 1990, Tables 1 and 3, pp. 207 and 208.

Notes: Pregnancy: Pregnancies are defined as the sum of births, abortions and miscarriages. Miscarriages are estimated as 20% of births and 10% of abortions. **Sexually experienced women:**The sexually experienced population was estimated by interpolating from sexual behavior data for 1971, 1976, 1982 and 1988. Data were extrapolated for 1989 and 1990 using the 1982–1988 trend.

FIGURE 30

Pregnancy rates also vary considerably by race and ethnicity.[155]

♦Black teenagers have a higher pregnancy rate than their Hispanic and white peers: Some 19% of all black women aged 15–19 become pregnant each year, compared with 13% of Hispanics and 8% of whites.

♦The higher rate among blacks is only partly due to the fact that they are more likely than whites to be sexually experienced. Even among those who have had intercourse, blacks are considerably more likely than whites and Hispanics to become pregnant, presumably because they are less likely to use a contraceptive or to use it effectively.

Adolescent Men

Since pregnancy data have been collected almost exclusively for women, it is easy to ignore male involvement. However, young women typically marry men who are three or more years older than they are,[156] so it is likely that the male partners of pregnant teenagers are also older than the women.

♦Only 26% of the men involved in the pregnancies among women under age 18 are estimated to have been that young; 35% are aged 18–19, and 39% are at least 20.[157]

♦These comparisons suggest that while 18% of 15–17-year-old women who have had intercourse become pregnant each year, only about 4% of sexually experienced men who are that young make a partner pregnant.[158]

Adolescent men may be less likely than adolescent women to be involved in a pregnancy, because many are having sex with even younger women, who are still experiencing lower fecundity in the years immediately following menarche, or because they are much less likely than young women to have sex frequently. Alternatively, the reports that higher proportions of young men than women have sex could be false.

Whatever the explanation, it cannot be assumed that the men involved in teenage pregnancies are comparable to the pregnant women. Nor can adolescent pregnancy continue to be viewed strictly as a teenage phenomenon. Age differences between partners raise concerns about how persuasive young women can be in insisting that their partners use condoms and how effective disease and pregnancy prevention programs can be if they focus only on teenagers and ignore their older partners.

Different Directions

Many of the milestones along the path to adulthood—completing education, finding full-time employment and getting married—now typically occur in the late teenage years or, more commonly, in the early

RISE WITH AGE

The oldest sexually experienced teenagers are the most likely to become pregnant.

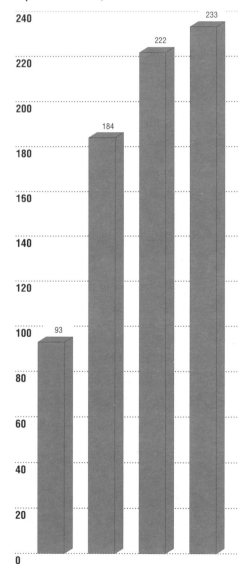

Pregnancies per 1,000 sexually experienced women, 1990

14 and younger	15–17	18–19	20–24
93	184	222	233

FIGURE 31

Sources: Births: National Center for Health Statistics, "Advance Report of Final Natality Statistics, 1990," *Monthly Vital Statistics Report,* Vol. 41, No. 9, Supplement, 1993, Table 2, p. 18. **Abortion, 1990:** S. K. Henshaw, "U.S. Teenage Pregnancy Statistics," AGI, New York, 1993. **Sexual activity data: 14 and younger:** AGI tabulations of data from the 1990 Youth Risk Behavior Survey; **15–24:** J. D. Forrest and S. Singh, "The Sexual and Reproductive Behavior of American Women, 1982–1988," *Family Planning Perspectives,* **22**:206–214, 1990, Tables 1 and 3, pp. 207 and 208.

Notes: Pregnancy: Pregnancies are defined as the sum of births, abortions and miscarriages. Miscarriages are estimated as 20% of births and 10% of abortions. **Sexually experienced women:** The sexually experienced population was estimated using the 1982–1988 trend. To estimate sexual experience for women under 15 years of age, data from the Youth Risk Behavior Survey (YRBS) were used. Because the YRBS reports higher levels of sexual activity than the National Survey of Family Growth (NSFG), YRBS estimates were deflated on the basis of the ratio of YRBS to NSFG figures on proportions of 18-year-old women who have had intercourse.

20s. On the other hand, a quarter of all young women have been pregnant by the time they turn 18, and half have had a pregnancy by age 21.[159]

♦ Young black women and teenagers who are poor or low-income are especially likely to become pregnant early in life.

♦ Typically, there is a gap of three years between first intercourse and first pregnancy among poor and low-income teenagers, compared with a gap of four and a half years among higher income adolescents.

♦ Similarly, blacks and Hispanics generally become pregnant less than three years after becoming sexually experienced, while whites wait more than four years.[160]

Unintended Pregnancies

Some 85% of teenage pregnancies are unintended.[161] Teenagers are not alone in experiencing high rates of unintended pregnancy, however; 55% of pregnancies among older women are unintended. As a result, teenagers account for only about a quarter of all accidental pregnancies annually.[162]

♦ Pregnancies among higher income teenagers are more likely to be unintended than are those among poor and low-income adolescents; among older women, by contrast, those with higher incomes are less likely to have an unintended pregnancy than are those who are poor or low-income.[163]

♦ Hispanic teenagers who become pregnant are somewhat more likely than blacks or whites to have wanted to get pregnant or at least not to have cared whether or not they became pregnant.[164]

♦ Whether an adolescent intends to become pregnant is strongly affected by whether she is married (Figure 32, page 43). Even among married teenagers, however, most pregnancies are unintended. And since so few teenagers are married, 60% of intended pregnancies among women under age 20 occur among unmarried women.[165]

Pregnancy rates among sexually experienced teenagers have declined substantially over the last two decades, but because the proportion of teenagers who are sexually experienced has grown, the overall teenage pregnancy rate has increased. One million young women become pregnant annually, the vast majority unintentionally. Older teenagers and adolescents who are poor or black are more likely to get pregnant than are their younger, more advantaged and white counterparts. The way in which teenagers resolve their pregnancies also differs by age, income status, race and ethnicity, and marital status.

DO THEY WANT TO GET PREGNANT?

Pregnancies among married teenagers are about five times as likely as those among unmarried teenagers to be intended.

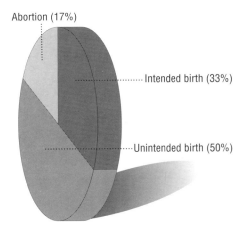

Pregnancy outcomes among married women aged 19 and younger, 1988: 180,000

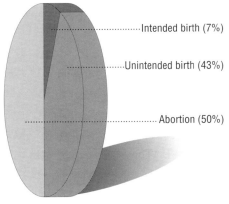

Pregnancy outcomes among unmarried women aged 19 and younger, 1988: 716,000

Sources: Number of births: National Center for Health Statistics, "Advance Report of Final Natality Statistics, 1988," *Monthly Vital Statistics Report,* Vol. 39, No. 4, Supplement, 1990, Table 2, p. 16. **Distribution of intended and unintended births:** AGI tabulations of data from the 1988 National Maternal and Infant Health Survey. **Abortions:** S. K. Henshaw, L. M. Koonin and J. C. Smith, "Characteristics of U.S. Women Having Abortions, 1987,"

Family Planning Perspectives, **23**:75–81, 1991, Table 3, p. 77; S. K. Henshaw, "Abortion Trends in 1987 and 1988: Age and Race," *Family Planning Perspectives,* **24**:85–87, 1992, Table 1, p. 69.

Note: Pregnancies do not include miscarriages. The 1987 distribution of marital status among women having abortions was applied to the 1988 number of abortions.

FIGURE 32

Outcomes of Adolescent Pregnancies

A woman can resolve a pregnancy in one of three ways: She can have an abortion; she can give birth and become a parent; or she can give birth and relinquish the baby for adoption. The overwhelming majority of teenagers choose either abortion or raising the child themselves. Since the late 1980s, the proportion of pregnant teenagers giving birth has increased slightly (Figure 33, page 44). About half of adolescent pregnancies end in birth, slightly over a third in abortion and the rest in miscarriage[166] (Figure 34, page 45). Although most adolescent pregnancies are unintended, teenagers account for fewer than a third of all unintended births, nonmarital births and abortions each year (Figure 35, page 46).

Abortion

In the years immediately following legalization of abortion in 1973, reported adolescent abortion rates increased considerably, and then were relatively stable until the late 1980s, even though a higher proportion of teenage women were becoming sexually active. Since 1980, however, abortion rates among sexually experienced adolescent women have declined steadily, both because a lower proportion of teenagers have become pregnant and because a lower proportion of pregnant teenagers have chosen to have an abortion (Figure 36, page 47). Adolescents account for roughly a quarter of all abortions performed annually.[167]

Terminating Unintended Pregnancies. The majority of unintended pregnancies among teenagers end in abortion.[168]

♦ In all, 53% of 15–19-year-old teenagers who experience unintended pregnancies have an abortion, compared with 47% of older women who have unintended pregnancies.

♦ Married teenagers are considerably less likely than their unmarried peers to terminate unintended pregnancies, perhaps because they have the support of a spouse and their family, or because married couples are more likely to be employed, have higher incomes and are more willing to have children than unmarried women and their partners.

♦ Still, about a quarter of unintended pregnancies among married adolescents end in abortion each year.[169]

In general, teenagers from families that are better off financially are more likely than those from poorer homes to terminate unintended pregnancies.[170]

HIGHER PROPORTION OF PREGNANT TEENAGERS GIVING BIRTH

Since 1988, the proportion of teenage pregnancies ending in birth rather than abortion has risen.

% of pregnancies among women aged 15–19 ending in birth

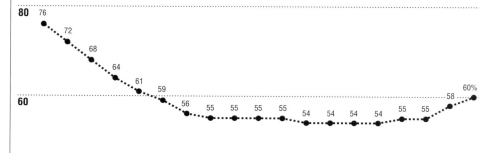

Sources: Births, 1972–1990: National Center for Health Statistics, "Advance Report of Final Natality Statistics," *Monthly Vital Statistics Report,* Vols. 23–41, Supplements, 1974–1993. **Abortions, 1973–1988:** S. K. Henshaw and J. Van Vort, eds., *Abortion Factbook, 1992 Edition: Readings, Trends and State and Local Data to 1988,* AGI, New York, 1992, Table 1, pp. 172–173; **1972, 1989–1990:** S. K. Henshaw, "U.S. Teenage Pregnancy Statistics," AGI, New York, 1993.

Note: Pregnancies do not include miscarriages.

FIGURE 33

♦ Nearly three-quarters of higher income teenagers who accidentally become pregnant have abortions, compared with fewer than half of those from poor or low-income families.[171]

♦ Those who are covered by Medicaid for the cost of their health care are considerably less likely to have abortions[172]—in part because most states do not pay for abortion services under Medicaid[173] (but all states pay for prenatal care and childbirth). The average cost of an outpatient, first-trimester abortion is $250.[174]

♦ Pregnant teenagers whose parents have more education are more likely than those with less-educated parents to end their pregnancies in abortion.[175]

♦ Those who have a stronger orientation toward the future also are relatively likely to choose abortion.[176]

Race and ethnicity make a difference. So does the age of the man involved in the pregnancy.

♦ Nearly 60% of white teenagers whose pregnancies were unintended choose abortion, compared with fewer than 50% of black and Hispanic adolescents.[177]

♦ Among pregnant women under age 18 whose male partners are also under 18, 61% have abortions, compared with 57% of those whose partners are 18–19, and 33% of those whose partners are aged 20 or older.[178]

Deciding on Abortion. Teenagers who have abortions most often cite their young age and low income as the reasons why they decided to end their pregnancies[179] (Figure 37, page 48).

Historically, states have required that parents give their consent before their minor child receives medical treatment. (In all but four states, the age of majority is 18.) There have long been exceptions to this rule, however, and many states now authorize minors to make their own decisions about reproductive health care, such as prenatal care, contraceptive services, and STD testing and treatment. Furthermore, no state specifically requires parental involvement for a minor to obtain these services. The trend in abortion law has been just the opposite, however.[180]

♦ Only three states—Connecticut, Maine and Wisconsin—and the District of Columbia have laws that allow a minor to consent to abortion services on her own. These states require counseling of the minor or strongly encourage her to involve her parents in her decision.

♦ On the other hand, 21 states have enacted statutes that require a minor either to have the consent of or to notify a parent (and in some cases, both parents) prior to having an abortion. In most of these states, a minor can avoid involving a parent by going to court and obtaining a

---

TEENAGE PREGNANCY OUTCOMES

Half of the more than 1 million pregnancies among adolescent women each year end in birth; a third end in abortion. Most of the births are unintended.

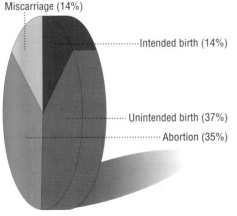

Miscarriage (14%)

Intended birth (14%)

Unintended birth (37%)

Abortion (35%)

Estimated pregnancies among women aged 19 and younger, 1990: 1,040,000

Sources: Births: National Center for Health Statistics, "Advance Report of Final Natality Statistics, 1990," *Monthly Vital Statistics Report*, Vol. 41, No. 9, Supplement, 1993, Table 2, p. 18. **Abortions:** S. K. Henshaw, "U.S. Teenage Pregnancy Statistics," AGI, New York, 1993. **Birth intention status:** AGI tabulations of data from the 1988 National Maternal and Infant Health Survey.

Notes: Miscarriages are estimated as 20% of births and 10% of abortions. To estimate the number of intended and unintended births, the distribution of births by intention status in 1988 was applied to the total number of births in 1990.

FIGURE 34

judge's authorization for an abortion. This legal option is not always known or understood by teenagers, however, and can lead to delay in obtaining an abortion or, by default, to an unintended birth.[181]

♦ In the remaining states, the law is silent on the issue of parents' role in a minor's access to abortion.

What Parents Know. Even in states where parental involvement is not mandated, six in 10 unmarried teenagers under age 18 having an abortion say at least one parent—usually their mother—knows of their decision to terminate a pregnancy[182] (Figure 38, page 49).

♦ The younger the teenager, the more likely she is to talk with at least one parent.

♦ Teenagers who consult their parents often say that they would not feel right keeping their pregnancy a secret from their parents, or that they need their parents' moral support and help in deciding what to do and how to get an abortion.

♦ Many young women who do not tell their parents about their pregnancy say they do not want to hurt or disappoint their parents or face their parents' anger.

Involvement of Male Partners. Teenagers who do not inform their parents about their pregnancy do talk to someone other than an abortion clinic staff member, most often their boyfriend, about their decision.[183]

♦ More than three-quarters of women under 18 having abortions talk over their decision with their boyfriend, who, in most

---

TEENAGERS A SMALL PART OF A LARGER PROBLEM

Teenagers account for fewer than a third of all abortions, nonmarital births and unintended births each year.

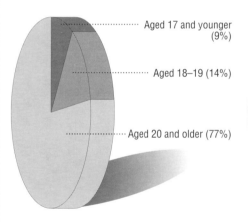

Aged 17 and younger (9%)

Aged 18–19 (14%)

Aged 20 and older (77%)

Abortions, 1990: 1,609,000

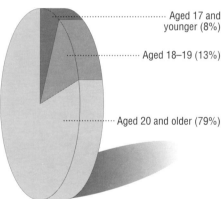

Aged 17 and younger (8%)

Aged 18–19 (13%)

Aged 20 and older (79%)

Unintended births, 1990: 1,796,000

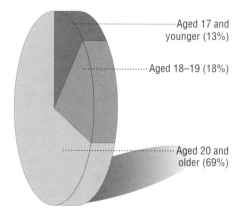

Aged 17 and younger (13%)

Aged 18–19 (18%)

Aged 20 and older (69%)

Nonmarital births, 1990: 1,165,000

Sources: Pregnancies and abortions: S. K. Henshaw, "U.S. Teenage Pregnancy Statistics," AGI, New York, 1993; other AGI unpublished data. **Births:** National Center for Health Statistics, "Advance Report of Final Natality Statistics, 1990," *Monthly Vital Statistics Report,* Vol. 41, No. 9, Supplement, 1993, Table 16, p. 33. **Birth intention status:** AGI tabulations of data from the 1988 National Maternal and Infant Health Survey.

Note: To estimate the number of intended and unintended births, the distribution of births by intention status in 1988 was applied to the total number of births in 1990.

FIGURE 35

cases, is the man involved in the pregnancy.

♦ Most consult their boyfriend even if their parents know about their decision to have an abortion.

♦ Half the young women have help from their boyfriend in paying for the abortion. (About two-fifths receive financial support from their parents, and about a quarter pay for the abortion themselves.)

Adoption

As childbearing outside marriage has become less stigmatized, the likelihood that a woman will place her baby for adoption has declined dramatically[184] (Figure 39, page 50).

♦ The decline has occurred almost exclusively among white women. Between 1982 and 1988, only 3% of never-married, non-Hispanic white women relinquished their

DECLINE IN TEENAGE ABORTION RATES

Since the late 1970s, the abortion rate has declined among sexually experienced teenagers.

Abortions per 1,000 women aged 15–19

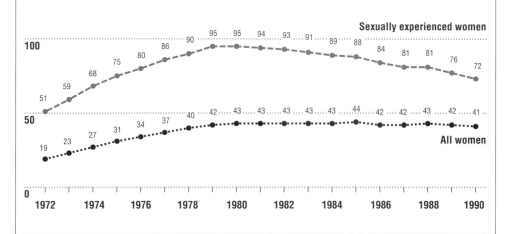

FIGURE 36

Sources: Abortions, 1973–1988: S. K. Henshaw and J. Van Vort, eds., *Abortion Factbook, 1992 Edition: Readings, Trends, and State and Local Data to 1988,* AGI, New York, 1992, Table 1, pp. 172–173; **1972, 1989–1990:** S. K. Henshaw, "U.S. Teenage Pregnancy Statistics," AGI, New York, 1993. **Sexually experienced women:** E. F. Jones et al., *Teenage Pregnancy in Industrialized Countries,* Yale University Press, New Haven and London, 1986, Table 3.5, p. 47; J. D. Forrest and S. Singh, "The Sexual and Reproductive Behavior of American Women, 1982–1988," *Family Planning Perspectives,* **22**:206–214, 1990, Tables 1 and 3, pp. 207 and 208.

Notes: Sexually experienced women: The sexually experienced population was estimated by interpolating from data for 1971, 1976, 1982 and 1988. To estimate sexual activity after 1988, data were extrapolated for 1989 and 1990 using the 1982–1988 trend.

Those who have a stronger orientation toward the future are relatively likely to choose abortion.

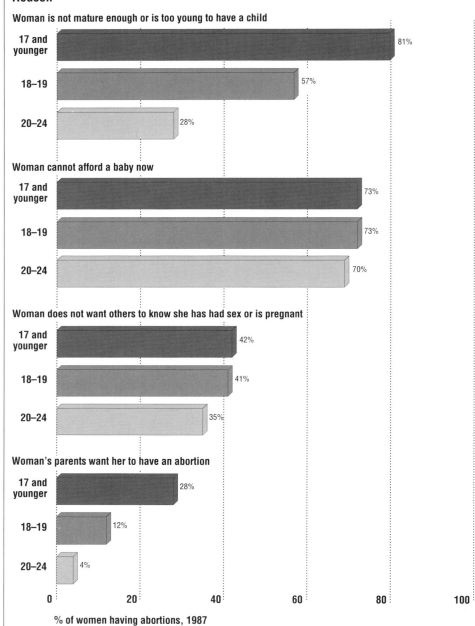

FACTORS IN ABORTION CHOICE

Teenagers who have abortions most commonly give their young age and low income as reasons for making that decision.

Reason

Woman is not mature enough or is too young to have a child

17 and younger	81%
18–19	57%
20–24	28%

Woman cannot afford a baby now

17 and younger	73%
18–19	73%
20–24	70%

Woman does not want others to know she has had sex or is pregnant

17 and younger	42%
18–19	41%
20–24	35%

Woman's parents want her to have an abortion

17 and younger	28%
18–19	12%
20–24	4%

0   20   40   60   80   100

% of women having abortions, 1987

Source: A. Torres and J. D. Forrest, "Why Do Women Have Abortions?" *Family Planning Perspectives,* **20**:169–176, 1988, Table 1, p. 170.

Note: The reasons given are not mutually exclusive. Most women gave multiple reasons.

FIGURE 37

infants for adoption, whereas 19% had done so during the period 1965–1972.

♦ Historically, black teenage women have rarely placed infants for adoption.

Births and Parenthood

Between the mid-1960s and the mid-

1980s, birthrates among sexually experienced teenagers declined. Since 1986, however, birthrates have been rising, especially among 18–19-year-olds[185] (Figure 40, page 51).

The increase has occurred among teenagers of all races, but has been espe-

% of women having abortions, 1990–1991

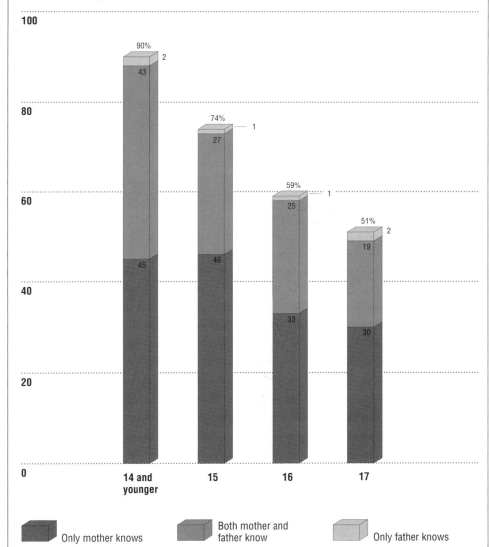

FIGURE 38

Only mother knows | Both mother and father know | Only father knows

Many young women who do not tell their parents about their pregnancy say they do not want to hurt or disappoint their parents or face their parents' anger.

Source: S. K. Henshaw and K. Kost, "Parental Involvement in Minors' Abortions Decisions," *Family Planning Perspectives*, **24**:196–207, 213, 1992, Table 8, p. 205.

cially pronounced among young Hispanic women.[186] The rise has occurred among sexually experienced teenagers and all adolescent women alike, which indicates that it reflects not only the higher proportions of teenagers having intercourse, but also the higher proportion of pregnant teenagers giving birth rather than having abortions.

♦ Of all births in the United States, 12% are to adolescents—4% to those under age 18 and 8% to 18–19-year-olds.[187]

♦ More adolescent women than teenage men become parents each year. In 1988, about 489,000 teenage women became mothers, but only 195,000 adolescent males became fathers[188] (Figure 41, page 52). The difference reflects that many of the fathers of babies born to adolescent women are not teenagers[189] (Figure 42, page 53).

♦ Although the recent increases in birth-

DECLINE IN ADOPTION

The chances that children of never-married women
will be placed for adoption have dropped.

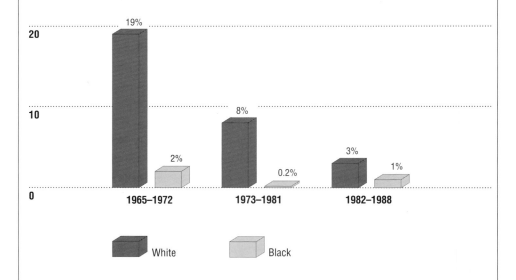

% of babies born to never-married women placed for adoption

Source: C. A. Bachrach, K. S. Stolley and K. A. London, "Relinquishment of Premarital Births: Evidence from National Survey Data," *Family Planning Perspectives*, **24**:27–32, 48, 1992, Table 1, p. 29.

Notes: In this figure, "white" is defined as "white, non-Hispanic," and "black" is defined as "black, non-Hispanic." Percentages are based on data from the 1982 and 1988 National Survey of Famliy Growth and refer to premarital births that had occurred to women who were aged 15–44 at either survey.

FIGURE 39

rates have been similar for black and white teenagers, black, as well as Hispanic, adolescents are substantially more likely than whites to give birth[190] (Figure 43, page 54).

♦ There is considerable variation in birthrates within racial and ethnic groups, however. On average, for example, 10% of Hispanic women aged 15–19 give birth each year; but only 3% of young women of Cuban descent, who tend to be among the most advantaged Hispanic group, have a baby, compared with 10–11% of teenagers of Mexican and Puerto Rican descent, who are more likely to be disadvantaged.[191]

Out-of-Wedlock Births. One of the most fundamental changes in patterns of childbearing and family structure over the last several decades has been the growing proportion of babies conceived and born

BIRTHRATES RISING

After a 15-year decline among sexually experienced teenagers, birthrates among both sexually experienced and all teenage women have begun to go up.

Births per 1,000 women aged 15–19

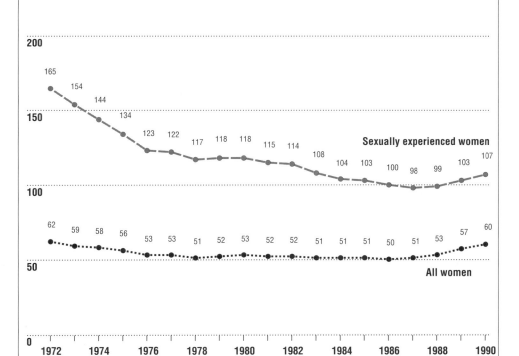

Sexually experienced women

All women

Sources: National Center for Health Statistics, "Advance Report of Final Natality Statistics, 1991," *Monthly Vital Statistics Report,* Vol. 42, No. 3, Supplement, 1993, Table 4, p. 20. **Sexual experience:** E. F. Jones et al., *Teenage Pregnancy in Industrialized Countries,* Yale University Press, New Haven and London, 1986, Table 3.5, p. 47; J. D. Forrest and S. Singh, "The Sexual and Reproductive Behavior of American Women, 1982–1988," *Family Planning Perspectives,* **22**: 206–214, 1990, Tables 1and 3, pp. 207 and 208.

Notes: Sexually experienced women: The sexually experienced population was estimated by interpolating from data for 1971, 1976, 1982 and 1988. To estimate sexual activity after 1988, data were extrapolated for 1989 and 1990 using the 1982–1988 trend.

FIGURE 40

outside marriage. The increase has occurred among women of all ages; it has been more rapid among older women than among teenagers. While most births to teenagers occur outside marriage, adolescents account for only 30% of all out-of-wedlock births, down from 50% in 1970.[192]

Among teenagers, there has been a dramatic shift in the pattern of first births[193] (Figure 44, page 55).

♦ In 1960–1964, 59% of first births to women aged 15–17 occurred among teenagers who had conceived outside marriage; 26% of young first-time mothers had married while pregnant, however, so that only a third of first births to women in this age-group occurred out of wedlock.

♦ By 1985–1989, 92% of first births to 15–17-year-olds occurred among women who had conceived outside marriage, and only 11% of new mothers had married while pregnant. Thus, 81% of first births

PARENTHOOD, BY GENDER

Fewer teenage men than women are parents; teenage fathers are older than teenage mothers.

Births to women and men 19 and younger, 1988

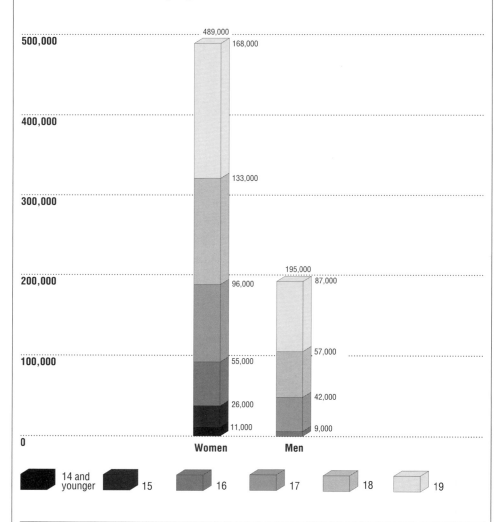

Sources: Women: National Center for Health Statistics, "Advance Report of Final Natality Statistics, 1988," *Monthly Vital Statistics Report,* Vol. 39, No. 4, Supplement, 1990, Table 2, p. 16. **Men:** AGI tabulations of data from the 1988 National Maternal and Infant Health Survey.

Note: When age of father was not reported on the birth certificate portion of the National Maternal and Infant Health Survey (NMIHS), the mother's report of father's age at the time of birth was calculated from the interview portion of the NMIHS. For men, the youngest age group is 16 and younger.

FIGURE 41

to women aged 15–17 in 1985–1989 occurred outside marriage.

♦ The same pattern is evident for 18–19-year-olds, although the proportion of first births occurring to unmarried women was lower (Figure 45, page 56).

Out-of-wedlock births account for nearly seven in 10 of all births to adolescent women.[194]

♦ In 1990, about 361,000 unmarried adolescent women gave birth.

♦ In that year, more than nine in 10 black mothers under 20 were unmarried when they gave birth, compared with fewer than six in 10 white teenagers (Figure 46, page 57).

♦ Among whites, the proportion of births that are out-of-wedlock declines sharply

> *More adolescent women than teenage men become parents each year....The difference reflects that many of the fathers of babies born to adolescent women are not teenagers.*

THE OLDER MAN

For a sizable minority of young women becoming mothers, the father of the baby is considerably older—by six years or more.

% of women giving birth who have partners at least six years older, 1988

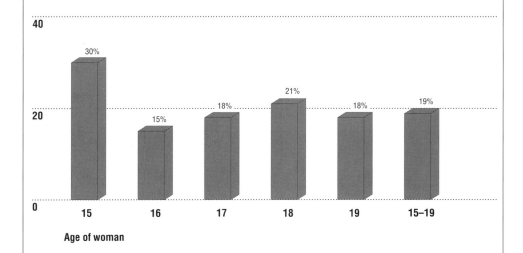

Age of woman

Source: AGI tabulations of data from the 1988 National Maternal and Infant Health Survey.

Note: When age of father was not reported on the birth certificate portion of the National Maternal and Infant Health

Survey (NMIHS), the mother's report of father's age at the time of birth was calculated from the interview portion of the NMIHS.

FIGURE 42

with age, but among blacks, it drops only slightly with increasing age, because marriage among blacks is less common.

♦ Nearly three-quarters of births to poor teenagers and to higher income teenagers occur out of wedlock, compared with slightly fewer than half of births to low-income teenagers.[195]

About a third of adolescent women marrying for the first time have a child or are pregnant, although the likelihood differs by race and age (Figure 47, page 57). The few black women who marry in their teenage years are much more likely than Hispanic and white brides to be mothers already or to be pregnant at their wedding.[196]

Childbearing is concentrated among teenagers who are poor or black.

RACIAL DIFFERENCES IN BIRTHRATES

At each age, young black and Hispanic women are more likely than white women to give birth.

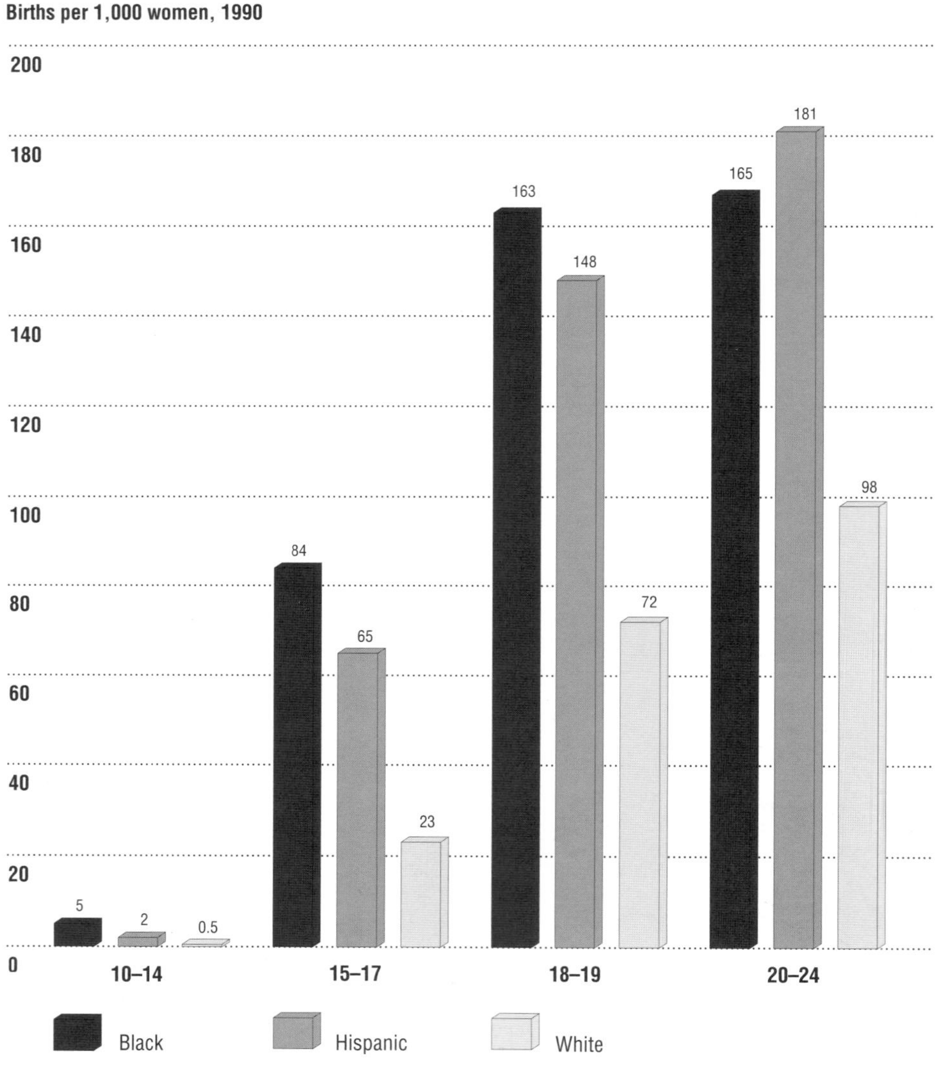

Births per 1,000 women, 1990

Age	Black	Hispanic	White
10–14	5	2	0.5
15–17	84	65	23
18–19	163	148	72
20–24	165	181	98

■ Black   ■ Hispanic   □ White

Sources: National Center for Health Statistics, "Advance Report of Final Natality Statistics, 1990," *Monthly Vital Statistics Report*, Vol. 41, No. 9, Supplement, 1993, Tables 3, 24 and 25, pp. 20, 40 and 41; F. W. Hollmann, "Estimates of the Population of the United States by Age, Sex, and Race," *Current Population Reports*, Series P-25, No. 1095, 1993, Table 1, p. 4.

Note: The data exclude New Hampshire and Oklahoma, which did not report Hispanic origin of mother on the birth certificate.

FIGURE 43

◆◆◆◆

Overwhelmingly, pregnant teenagers either have an abortion or give birth and raise the child themselves; adoption is rare. White adolescents and those from more advantaged backgrounds generally elect to terminate their pregnancies. Childbearing, meanwhile, is concentrated among teenagers who are poor or black. Young mothers, then, tend already to be disadvantaged at the time of their child's birth. They also are at risk of falling further behind their more advantaged peers who have chosen to postpone childbearing.

BIRTHS OUT OF WEDLOCK

The percentage of first births to teenagers that occur out of wedlock has increased dramatically since the early 1960s—from 33% to 81%.

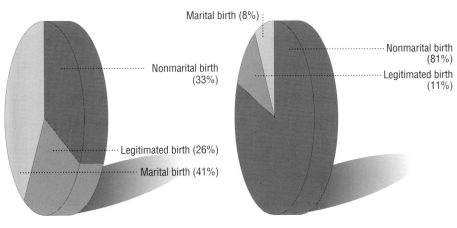

Marital birth (8%)

Nonmarital birth (33%)

Legitimated birth (26%)

Marital birth (41%)

Nonmarital birth (81%)

Legitimated birth (11%)

First births to women aged 15–17, 1960–1964: 731,000

First births to women aged 15–17, 1985–1989: 673,000

Source: A. Bachu, "Fertility of American Women: June 1990," *Current Population Reports,* Series P-20, No. 452, 1991, Table E, p. 7.

Note: "Nonmarital birth" denotes conception and birth outside marriage. "Legitimated birth" denotes conception outside marriage and birth in marriage.

FIGURE 44

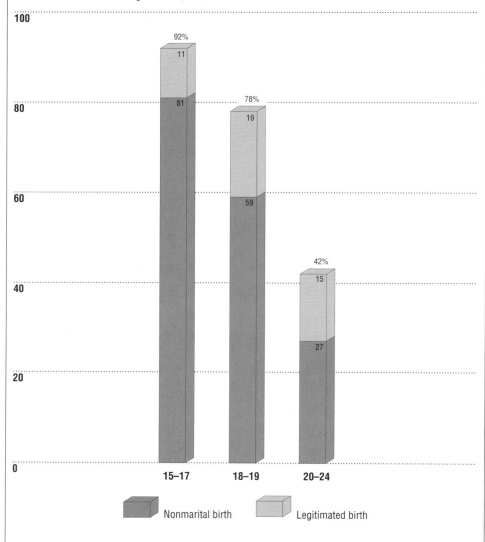

OUT-OF-WEDLOCK BIRTHS, BY AGE

The younger the mother, the more likely it is that she first conceived
and gave birth outside marriage.

% of first births to women aged 15–24, 1985–1989

Source: A. Bachu, "Fertility of American Women: June 1990," *Current Population Reports*, Series P-20, No. 454, 1991, Table E, p. 7.

Note: "Nonmarital birth" denotes conception and birth outside marriage. "Legitimated birth" denotes conception outside marriage and birth in marriage.

FIGURE 45

NONMARITAL BIRTHS, BY RACE

Births to black teenagers are more likely to be nonmarital than are births to whites.

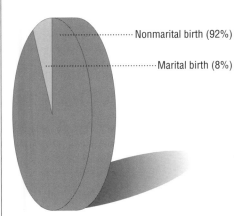

Nonmarital birth (92%)

Marital birth (8%)

Nonmarital birth (57%)

Marital birth (43%)

**All births to black women aged
19 and younger, 1990: 158,000**

**All births to white women aged
19 and younger, 1990: 359,500**

Source: National Center for Health Statistics, "Advance Report of Final Natality Statistics, 1990," *Monthly Vital Statistics Report,* Vol. 41, No. 9, Supplement, 1993, Table 2, pp. 18–19, and Table 16, p. 33.

Notes: In this figure, the terms "black" and "white" refer to race; Hispanics are categorized by race, not by ethnicity. "Marital birth" denotes conception and birth in marriage, as well as conception outside marriage and birth in marriage.

FIGURE 46

GETTING MARRIED, WITH CHILD

Some 31% of women who marry at age 19 or younger already have a child or are pregnant.

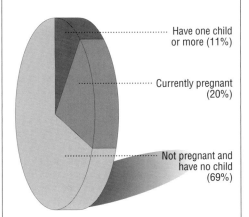

Have one child
or more (11%)

Currently pregnant
(20%)

Not pregnant and
have no child
(69%)

**Women under age 25 in 1988 who first married
at age 19 or younger**

Source: AGI tabulations of data from the 1988 National Survey of Family Growth.

Note: "Currently pregnant" women are those whose first baby was born seven months or less after their first marriage.

FIGURE 47

Adolescent Mothers and Their Children

One in four black women and one in seven white women are already mothers at age 19.[197] Young mothers are more likely than other teenagers, including those who become pregnant but have abortions, to come from economically and socially disadvantaged backgrounds (Figure 48, page 58).

♦ Poor and low-income teenagers accounted for 83% of women 15–19 who gave birth in 1988, although they constituted only 38% of all women in that age-group. By contrast, higher income teenagers made up 62% of all women 15–19, yet represented just 17% of those who gave birth.[198]

♦ Nearly 60% of teenagers who become mothers are living in poverty at the time of the birth.[199]

♦ Nearly 60% of adolescents giving birth for the first time have their delivery fees covered by public funds, usually Medicaid (Figure 49, page 59). Even so, teenagers accounted for only about a quarter of all deliveries covered by Medicaid in 1988.[200]

♦ Adolescent mothers are more likely than other teenagers to come from single-parent households.[201]

♦ Blacks and Hispanics, who are disproportionately poor or low-income, have a higher likelihood than whites of becoming adolescent mothers.[202]

Support for Adolescent Mothers

Because of their youth and disadvantaged background, teenage mothers are more likely than women who postpone childbearing to rely on their families and public assistance programs to cover the costs of raising a child and to enable them to complete their education and find employment. Even with this help, young parents are not always successful in reaching these goals.

Living with Their Parents. Pregnant teenagers and adolescent parents, most of whom are not married, often live with their parents.

♦ Almost three-quarters of pregnant teenagers under age 18 live with one or both of their parents.

♦ Even six months after giving birth, about 60% of young mothers aged 15–17 are still living at home.

♦ Young black mothers are more likely than Hispanics and whites to continue to live at home, usually in a single-parent household headed by their mother.[203]

While living at home can provide teenagers with crucial support during pregnancy and after the child is born, it may delay the assumption of other adult responsibilities, as well as hinder the role of the baby's father.

WHO GOES ON TO GIVE BIRTH?

Teenagers who give birth are much more likely to come from poor families than are teenagers who have an abortion or teenagers in general.

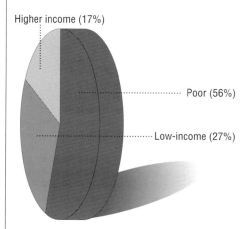

Higher income (17%)
Poor (56%)
Low-income (27%)

Women aged 15–19 who gave birth, 1988: 478,000

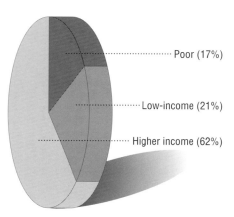

Poor (17%)
Low-income (21%)
Higher income (62%)

All women aged 15–19, 1988: 8,754,000

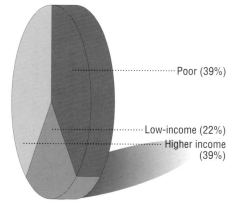

Poor (39%)
Low-income (22%)
Higher income (39%)

Women aged 15–19 who had an abortion, 1988: 393,000

Sources: Births: AGI tabulations of data from the 1988 National Maternal and Infant Health Survey. **Abortions:** AGI tabulations from a 1987 AGI survey of 9,480 women having abortions, reported in S. K. Henshaw, "Abortion Tends in 1987 and 1988: Age and Race," *Family Planning Perspectives,* **24**:85–87, Table 1, p.87. **All women:** Estimated by AGI from M. S. Littman and E. F. Baugher, "Poverty in the United States: 1988 and 1989," *Current Population Reports,* Series P-60, No. 171, Table 25, p. 191; Table 31, p. 249.

Notes: The proportion of abortions by income level in 1987 was applied to the total number of abortions in 1988. In this figure, for women having births and abortions, "poor" is defined by an annual family income under $12,000; "low-income" is defined by a family income of $12,000–$24,999; "higher income" means a family income of $25,000 or more.

FIGURE 48

Public Assistance. Teenage mothers are more likely than older mothers to need the support of public assistance.

♦ Some 25% of adolescent mothers receive public assistance by the time they reach their early 20s, compared with 19% of women who first give birth in their early 20s.[204]

♦ As teenage mothers get older, many move off public assistance;[205] even in their late 20s and early 30s, however, women who became mothers when they were teenagers are more likely to be on public assistance than are those who first gave birth when they were 20–24.[206]

♦ An estimated 53% of funds dispersed by the Aid to Families with Dependent Children (AFDC) program, the most common form of welfare, go to families formed by a teenage birth.[207]

Child Support. As rates of divorce and out-of-wedlock childbearing have risen over the last two decades, child support has become increasingly critical to the well-being of children.[208]

♦ Between 1979 and 1988, the number of women under age 30 with a child whose father was not living in the house rose 23% to 3.2 million.

♦ Yet, only a third of women under 30 raising children apart from the children's fathers received any child support in 1987.

♦ Child support makes up a larger proportion of income among women under age 30 than among older women, but the absolute dollar level of child support is lowest for young women. In 1987, the average annual payment received by mothers under 30 from their children's father was only $1,946, but it amounted to about 22% of their total monetary income.

♦ In most cases, the fathers of babies born to teenagers, though older than the mothers, are still in their teens or early 20s, when their earning power, and therefore their ability to provide support for their children, is low.[209]

A Matter of Timing

As the timing of adolescence and adulthood has changed, so has the timing of childbearing. In 1965, for example, teenagers accounted for 37% of all new mothers, while women aged 25 or older accounted for only 17%. By 1990, howev-er, only 23% of first births were to teenagers, and the proportion to women at least 25 had climbed to 45%. The shift toward delayed childbearing occurred among whites and blacks alike.[210]

As it is increasingly the norm for young women to delay childbearing, those teenagers who do become parents are increasingly differentiated from their peers. Growing proportions of advantaged women have been postponing childbearing to obtain more education and to advance their careers, thereby widening the gap between themselves and women who drop out of school or postpone their education and job advancement to have children. As the qualifications for good jobs rise, teenage mothers who fail to finish school have more difficulty finding gainful employment. Although many teenage parents eventually regain some of their initial disadvantage in school, employment and income, they seldom reach the level of their peers who delay childbearing.

Educational Attainment. Teenage mothers obtain less education than their peers who postpone childbearing.

♦ About 70% of women who give birth as teenagers finish high school by the time they are 35–39, compared with more than 90% of older mothers.

♦ Moreover, women who postpone childbearing are far more likely than those who first give birth as teenagers to go to college[211] (Figure 50, page 60).

Often, women who drop out of school and give birth as teenagers were not doing well in school even before the pregnancy occurred. In fact, many dropped out of school before they became pregnant. It appears that in terms of educational achievement, dropping out of school, not having a baby, is the key factor that sets adolescent mothers behind their peers.[212] If a pregnant teenager does drop out, it is unlikely that she will return to school before her children are in school.[213]

Adolescent mothers who stay in school are almost as likely eventually to graduate (73%) as women who do not become mothers while in high school (77%). In contrast, only about 30% of women who drop out of high school either before or after their baby's birth eventually graduate.[214]

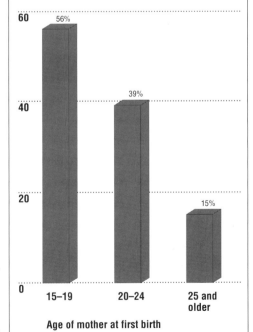

THE YOUNG AND FINANCIAL HELP

Younger mothers are more likely than others to need public assistance to pay for their delivery coverage.

% of mothers using public assistance for delivery coverage, 1988

Age of mother at first birth	%
15–19	56%
20–24	39%
25 and older	15%

Source: AGI tabulations of data from the 1988 National Maternal and Infant Health Survey.

Note: Public assistance includes Medicaid, Indian Health Services and other government assistance.

FIGURE 49

Timing of a Second Birth. Having a second birth within a few years of the first can be a barrier to completing high school.[215] While a young mother may be able to make certain life-course transitions if she has one child—such as finishing school and obtaining an entry-level job—those tasks become considerably more difficult if she has more than one child. Teenagers often have short intervals between their first and second births,[216] particularly compared with older mothers.[217]

♦ Some 19% of adolescents who become mothers at ages 15–17 and 25% of those who are aged 18–19 when they first give birth have a second child within two years.

♦ Closely spaced births early in a woman's life contribute to deficits in her education and employment, and increase her welfare dependency.

Divorce. Teenage mothers are not only more likely than other young women to have grown up in a single-parent household, they are also more likely to end their own marriage in divorce.[218]

♦ The younger a couple is when they marry, the more likely they are to divorce.

♦ Nearly a third of first marriages among teenagers end in divorce within five years, compared with 15% among couples who delay marriage until they are 23–29.

HOW MUCH EDUCATION DO THEY GET?

Over 70% of teenage mothers complete high school, but they are less likely than older mothers to go on to college.

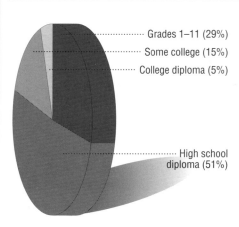

Grades 1–11 (29%)
Some college (15%)
College diploma (5%)
High school diploma (51%)

Women aged 35–39 in 1987 who gave birth at age 19 or younger

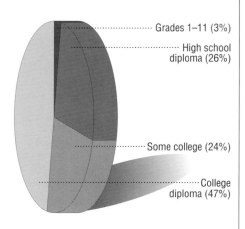

Grades 1–11 (3%)
High school diploma (26%)
Some college (24%)
College diploma (47%)

Women aged 35–39 in 1987 who gave birth at age 25 or older

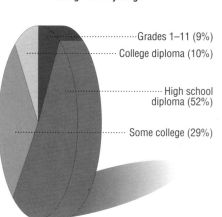

Grades 1–11 (9%)
College diploma (10%)
High school diploma (52%)
Some college (29%)

Women aged 35–39 in 1987 who gave birth at age 20–24

Source: AGI tabulations of data from the 1987 National Survey of Families and Households.

Note: "Some college" includes those with two-year or associate degrees.

FIGURE 50

Income. In general, young women who begin childbearing in their teens have lower future family incomes than those who postpone their first birth (Figure 51, page 61). The lower family income is due primarily to adolescent mothers' low educational attainment, their large family size and the fact that they are often unmarried.[219]

Childbearing and Prior Disadvantage

Teenage mothers are more likely than women who do not have a child before age 20 to be poor later in their lives[220] (Figure 52, page 62).

♦ Some 28% of women who become mothers as teenagers are poor in their 20s and early 30s.

♦ Only 7% of women who first give birth after adolescence are poor at those ages.

A continuing question is the degree to which teenage mothers' subsequent poverty is the result of early childbearing and the extent to which it is attributable to their prior economic and social disad-

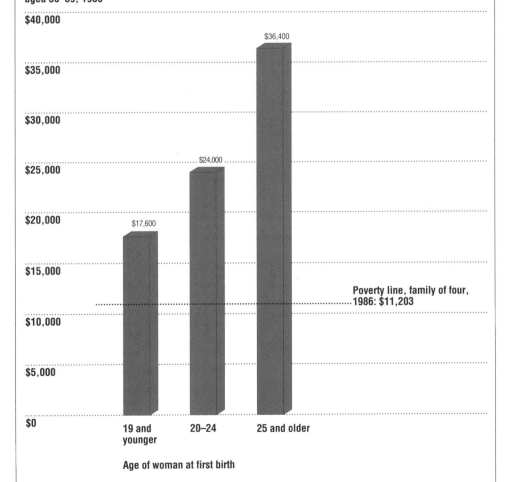

TEENAGE MOTHERS' INCOME IN LATER LIFE

Women who give birth as teenagers eventually have a median family income well above poverty, though lower than that of women who are older at first birth.

Median family income of women aged 30–39, 1986

$40,000

$36,400

$35,000

$30,000

$25,000 — $24,000

$20,000 — $17,600

$15,000

Poverty line, family of four, 1986: $11,203

$10,000

$5,000

$0

| 19 and younger | 20–24 | 25 and older |

Age of woman at first birth

Sources: Income: AGI tabulations of data from the 1987 National Survey of Families and Households. **Poverty line:** U.S. Bureau of the Census, "Poverty in the United States: 1987," *Current Population Reports*, Series P-60, No. 163, 1989, Table A-2, p. 157.

FIGURE 51

vantage. Their initial disadvantage, rather than having a baby, is itself a major reason that adolescent mothers are poor later in their lives. Overall, 16% of women who were adolescent mothers would have been poor in their 20s and 30s even if they had not begun childbearing as teenagers. Nevertheless, once their initial disadvantage has been accounted for, early childbearing still has a lasting impact on the lives and future opportunities of young mothers and their children.

Children of Adolescent Mothers

Children of teenage mothers do less well on indicators of good health and social and economic well-being than do children of older parents, which again largely reflects the young mothers' economic and social disadvantage prior to childbearing, rather than their young age per se. With extra support and access to good health care, birth outcomes among teenagers need not be com-

promised, and some research suggests that in certain cases, adolescent childbearing may have better health outcomes than childbearing among older women.[221]

Health Status. From a purely biological perspective, the late teenage years may be the optimal time to give birth, assuming a young woman receives high-quality prenatal and delivery care.[222] In reality, however, a third of pregnant teenagers receive inadequate prenatal care—twice the proportion for the average woman giving birth.[223]

♦ The younger a woman is, the less likely she is to receive prenatal care in the first trimester of her pregnancy.[224]

♦ The lack of early prenatal care occurs across racial and ethnic groups.[225]

♦ In contrast to patterns among older women, pregnant teenagers from higher income families are less likely than teenagers from poor families to receive prenatal care in the first or second trimester.[226]

Largely because of their lack of adequate prenatal care, teenagers are more likely than older women to have children whose health is compromised at birth.

♦ Low birth weight, an important contributor to infant mortality and future health problems, is more common among the infants of teenagers than among babies born to women in their 20s.

♦ Among both black and white adolescents, the youngest mothers are the most likely to bear underweight babies; but at all ages, black teenagers are considerably more likely than whites to have low-birth-weight babies.[227]

♦ Poverty status is one of the strongest predictors of low birth weight, especially among teenage mothers.[228]

♦ Black teenagers are more likely than whites and Hispanics to have a premature birth.[229]

Furthermore, babies born to young mothers are more likely than those born to older mothers to have health problems during childhood and to be hospitalized[230] (Figure 53, page 63).

Living Arrangements. As single parenthood and divorce have become more common, the living arrangements of children have changed markedly. Approximately

---

COMPOUNDING DISADVANTAGE

Because most teenage mothers come from disadvantaged backgrounds, 28% are poor in later life. Theoretically, had they delayed their first birth to age 20 or older, an estimated 16% would be poor; in fact, however, only 7% of women who delay childbearing are poor later on, demonstrating that the initial disadvantage of teenage mothers is compounded by the early birth.

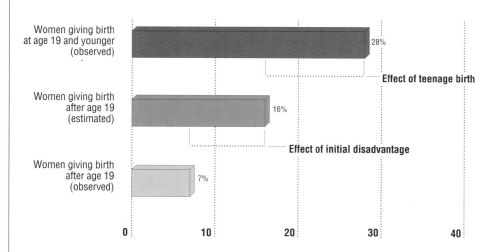

% of women aged 21–33 in 1987 who are poor

Sources: Women giving birth at age 19 and younger (observed) and **women giving birth after age 19 (estimated):** S. D. Hoffman, E. M. Foster and F. F. Furstenberg, Jr., "Reevaluating the Costs of Teenage Childbearing," *Demography,* **30**: 1–13, 1993, Table 3, p. 7. **Women giving birth after age 19 (observed):** Tabulations by S. D. Hoffman of data from the Panel Study of Income Dynamics.

Notes: Data are based on pairs of sisters aged 21–33 in 1987 who grew up in similar family and socioeconomic circumstances. **Estimated women giving birth after age 19 (observed)** who are poor at ages 21–33 were calculated by a fixed-effects model that contrasts the sister who had a teenage birth with the sister who did not.

FIGURE 52

half of all children in the United States today will spend some time living in a single-parent family.[231]

♦ About half of children under age six who were born to women younger than 18 live with only one parent, usually their mothers, compared with a quarter of those born to women in their early 20s.[232]

♦ Some 75% of black children under age six in 1987 who were born to teenagers lived with a single parent, compared with 44% of Hispanic children and 37% of white children born to teenage mothers.[233]

Cognitive Development. Children of teenage mothers consistently score lower than children of older mothers on measures of cognitive development. These results are not a direct consequence of the mother's young age at birth, but of the fact that younger mothers are more likely than others to be single parents, to have a large family and, most important, to have low educational attainment.[234] Rather than declining over time, the educational deficits of children born to adolescent mothers appear to accumulate, causing the child to fall further behind in school as he or she grows older.[235]

♦♦♦♦

Teenagers who become parents are disadvantaged, economically, educationally and socially, even before they have children, which is a major reason that adolescent parents tend to be poor later in their lives and to have less education and less-stable marriages. Nevertheless, early childbearing often compounds these initial disadvantages and makes it more difficult for young parents to keep pace with their peers who do not become parents in their teenage years. Young people who become parents very early in their lives need far more intensive interventions than other teenagers if they are to overcome these problems.

BABY'S HEALTH

Babies born to young mothers are more likely to have health problems during childhood and more likely to be hospitalized than are those born to older mothers.

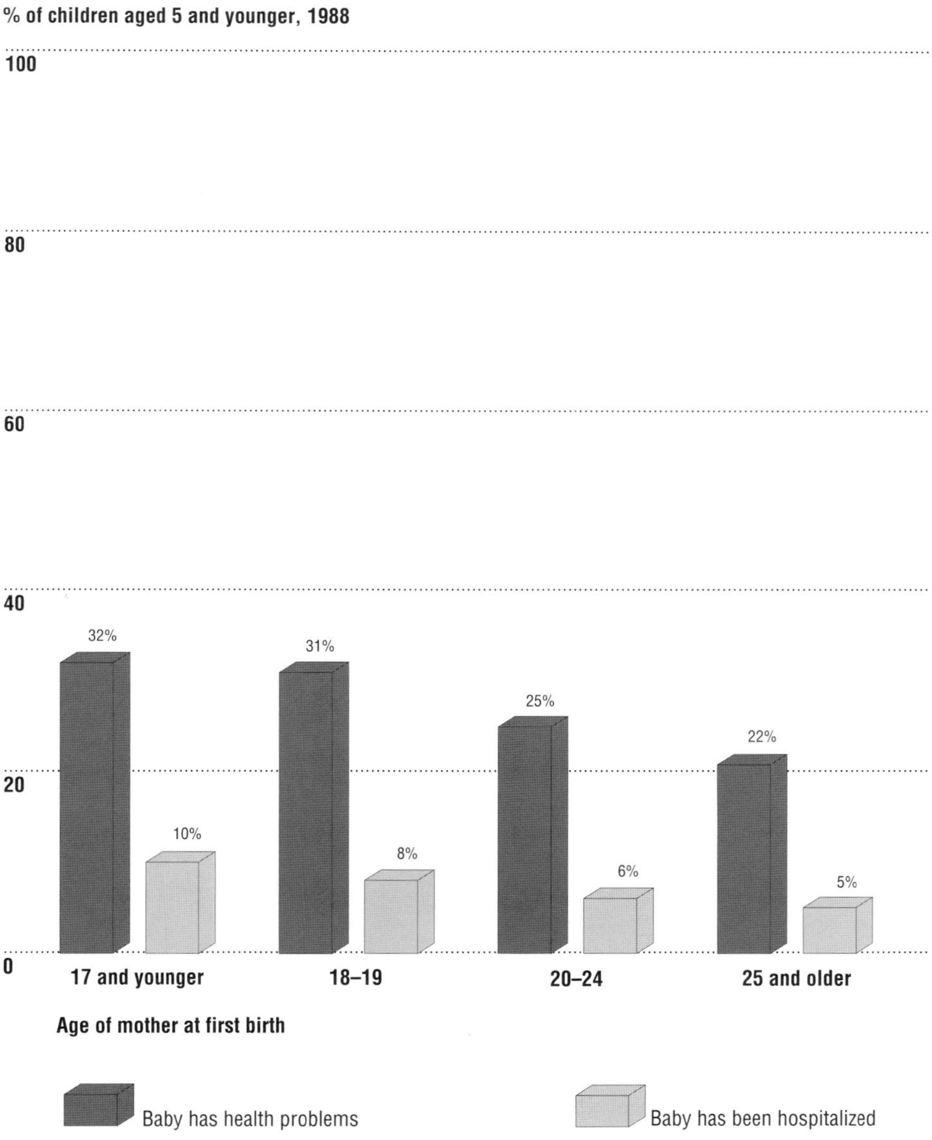

% of children aged 5 and younger, 1988

 Baby has health problems

 Baby has been hospitalized

Age of mother at first birth

	17 and younger	18–19	20–24	25 and older
Baby has health problems	32%	31%	25%	22%
Baby has been hospitalized	10%	8%	6%	5%

Source: AGI tabulations of data from the 1988 National Health Interview Survey.

Note: Health problems are defined by at least one caretaker's report that the child is less healthy than others, accident-prone or seriously ill, or has a delay in development. Hospitalizations refer to episodes in the 12 months prior to the survey.

FIGURE 53

Organized Responses to Adolescent Sexual and Reproductive Behavior

Parents and other adults have long tried to influence and control the sexual behavior of adolescents, especially young women, through admonitions, curfews, limitations on dating and forced marriage. The last two decades have seen the proliferation of organized interventions that parallel and supplement individual efforts to reduce teenage sexual activity and its negative consequences. Many of these interventions have focused either on trying to persuade adolescents, particularly young women, to abstain from sexual activity or on providing remedial services to pregnant teenagers and adolescent parents. Both of these approaches have instinctual appeal, but neither has been effective enough or perhaps intensive enough to have a major impact. On the other hand, there is evidence that some programs have succeeded in reducing levels of unprotected sexual behavior and pregnancy among young people who participate in them. The most effective programs typically combine innovative instructional techniques with information about methods to prevent pregnancy and STD transmission; some also facilitate adolescents' access to contraceptive services. Such programs are still relatively rare, however, and have yet to be implemented on a national scale.

Different Approaches

Programs designed to provide special services to pregnant teenagers who decide to give birth are perhaps the oldest form of organized intervention. Originally, these programs primarily entailed providing residential care for pregnant young women outside their home communities until they gave birth and, usually, relinquished their babies for adoption. As it has become the norm for pregnant adolescents to continue to live at home, attend school and keep their babies, these programs have evolved. They now concentrate on providing both necessary medical services, to ensure that young women receive adequate prenatal care so they will have healthy birth outcomes, and support services, to help adolescent mothers stay in school and learn skills they need as parents. Not all pregnant adolescents have access to coordinated services and support, however, because these programs are quite intensive and therefore costly.

Meanwhile, many family planning clinics and almost all school systems now offer sex education aimed at increasing young people's knowledge about reproduction. Some of these programs also provide information about contraception and STD transmission, and include lessons in communication skills. Programs associated with family planning clinics facilitate teenagers' access to medical contraceptive services, and a few schools have opened clinics that provide contraceptive and STD services or have implemented programs to make condoms available to students.

During the last decade, policies and programs designed to encourage abstinence among unmarried teenagers have become increasingly popular. Some of these programs have attempted to accomplish this objective by giving young people encouragement, offering moral support and teaching interpersonal skills to resist pressures to become sexually active.[236] Others have sought to convince teenagers that sex before marriage is immoral and have emphasized the negative consequences of sexual intercourse, while occasionally withholding or distorting information about the availability and effectiveness of contraceptives.[237]

On a broader scale, community and service organizations have implemented interventions aimed at increasing the life options of disadvantaged young people through, for example, role models and mentoring, community service projects, job training and activities aimed at reducing risky behaviors. Such interventions are expected indirectly to reduce levels of unintended teenage pregnancy and childbearing and sexually transmitted infections, in the belief that teenagers who are more positive about their futures are less likely to participate in risk-taking behaviors, including risky sexual practices.

Several model communitywide programs for high-risk, inner-city populations have linked substance abuse prevention with delinquency prevention, pregnancy prevention or educational achievement.[238]

Difficulty in Evaluating Programs

The numerous programs designed to address teenage sexual and reproductive behavior differ widely in content, type of intervention, group served, and breadth and comprehensiveness of their focus. Yet, very few of them have been evaluated, and even fewer have been evaluated adequately.

♦ Many programs do not have sufficient funding to support both program activities and evaluation, or have not been in existence long enough to be evaluated.

♦ It is frequently difficult to get support from communities and schools for evaluations that include asking teenagers about sexual behavior.

♦ Some programs are run by individuals who are confident about the impact of their activities and do not see the need for formal evaluation.

The focus here is primarily on programs that have been evaluated in a formal way; in some instances, new or promising program approaches for which no formal evaluations are available are also mentioned. For the most part, evaluations of pregnancy and STD prevention programs have attempted to measure change in adolescents' knowledge and attitudes regarding sexuality and reproduction, as well as change in their behavior—specifically, whether they delay the initiation of sexual intercourse and increase contraceptive use when they do have sex. Ultimately, programs that succeed in achieving these goals should lead to reduced levels of pregnancies, births and STDs among teenagers. This leap in expectations is not always borne out by those programs with adequate evaluations, however.

♦ In some cases, expectations may be too high. Education alone is not sufficient to change behavior deeply ingrained by one's cultural upbringing, the pressure of one's peers and the media.

♦ Even programs that have been successful in delaying the initiation of sexual activity and increasing reported contraceptive use among participants have not shown significant declines in teenage pregnancy rates.

♦ Intervention programs and their evaluations usually focus on short-term behavior changes. Thus, short delays in the initiation of intercourse or greater contraceptive use following an intervention that is not sustained in the long run may not be sufficient to significantly lower teenage pregnancy rates, given a typical span of eight years between the initiation of intercourse and marriage.

There are a number of problems associated with evaluation of pregnancy and STD prevention programs. Foremost among these are difficulties in obtaining valid outcome measures and in designing evaluations that can actually assess program effectiveness.

In terms of outcome, most evaluations rely on reports from teenagers themselves regarding levels of sexual activity, contraceptive use, pregnancy, abortion and STDs—all of which are difficult to measure, whether a program is in place or not. Alternatively, some evaluations use external data, countywide birthrates and abortion rates or estimated schoolwide pregnancy rates to measure program effectiveness. Schoolwide rates have been shown to fluctuate widely from year to year,[239] however, and countywide rates may be based on a pool of adolescents that is much larger than the group of teenagers participating in the program, which would dilute the effect of a program operating in only one school. In addition, because abortion data are usually reported according to the county in which the procedure occurs, it is difficult to calculate adolescent abortion rates according to county of residence.[240]

In terms of evaluation design, most studies attempt to compare program participants with a control group, such as students from other classrooms, other schools or other counties. Such comparisons, however, are fraught with difficulties.

♦ Control students usually receive some sort of sex education.

♦ Community messages about sexual behavior may reach both participants and controls.

It is frequently difficult to get support from communities and schools for evaluations that include asking teenagers about sexual behavior.

♦ Media events or heightened public discussion of AIDS may have an unmeasured impact on the behavior being evaluated.

♦ Unless participants are randomly assigned to program and control groups, teenagers opting for the program may be self-selected or selected by their parents or program staff because they have special needs. Even if the program has an effect, members of the control group may do well because they were better off to begin with.

Despite these limitations, program evaluations can be extremely useful in gauging the effectiveness of different program approaches. Those that have been done carefully provide insight into what strategies work well with adolescents.

Pregnancy and STD Prevention Programs

Increasing Knowledge and Skills. Perhaps the most common intervention, and the one that reaches the most young people, is classroom instruction in schools that is designed to increase teenagers' knowledge about sexuality.

♦ In the late 1980s, 76% of young women aged 15–19[241] and 75% of young men in that age-group[242] reported that before age 18, they had received some formal instruction related to methods of birth control.

♦ Some 79% of the young women (and 81% of the young men) reported receiving formal instruction about STDs.[243]

♦ Currently, 46 states and the District of Columbia mandate or recommend that schools provide sexuality education, while all 50 states and the District of Columbia mandate or recommend that schools provide AIDS education.[244] States are more likely, however, to require (as opposed to recommend) AIDS education than sex education.[245] But AIDS instruction is often less than candid about sexual transmission.

While traditional sex education has been successful in achieving the limited goal of increasing knowledge,[246] students do not appear to change their sexual behavior or increase their use of contraceptives unless the program provides specific information on how to resist sexual pressures and how to prevent pregnancy and disease.[247]

♦ When sexuality education includes explicit discussion of contraceptive methods and prevention of STDs, it increases students' knowledge of the effectiveness of different methods for preventing pregnancy and disease transmission, and sometimes raises contraceptive use among program participants.

♦ High school students who have received AIDS education are more knowledgeable about HIV transmission than are students who have not received such education, and in some cases are significantly less likely to participate in risky sexual behaviors.[248]

Curricula have been designed that combine sexuality education with interactive instruction emphasizing values and norms for responsible behavior and decision making so that students learn the communication skills needed to say "no" or "not yet" to sexual intercourse or unprotected sex. Some of the school-based programs that use this approach have had positive effects on participants' behavior.[249]

♦ Students delay the initiation of sexual intercourse. One study, for example, estimated that participants postponed sexual activity for seven months.[250]

♦ Participants become more likely to use condoms and other contraceptives. Three programs that were evaluated reported that 13–50% more participants than controls use contraceptives.[251]

♦ Higher proportions of participants than of controls were in monogamous relationships, and smaller proportions had high-risk partners, after the intervention.[252]

Not all school-based interventions report significant changes, however. To better understand why some programs are successful, while others are not, a panel of experts reviewed all published evaluations of school-based pregnancy and STD prevention programs. The results of this review suggest that characteristics of a program's curriculum and instructional techniques may determine its effectiveness. Successful interventions share a number of characteristics, including the following:

"(a) theoretical grounding in social learning or social influence theories,

(b) a narrow focus on reducing specific sexual risk-taking behaviors,

(c) experiential activities to convey the information on the risks of unprotected sex and how to avoid those risks and to personalize that information,

(d) instruction on social influences and pressures,

(e) reinforcement of individual values and group norms against unprotected sex that are age and experience appropriate, and

(f) activities to increase relevant skills and confidence in those skills." [253]

Service organizations and community agencies—such as Girls, Inc.; Boys Clubs; the Association of Junior Leagues; the American Red Cross; the Young Women's Christian Association; and churches—frequently offer after-school and summer programs that focus on increasing the life options of disadvantaged youth and on preventing risk-taking behaviors among teenagers; many include sexuality education and sexual decision making. These programs, particularly the components focused on pregnancy prevention, have had mixed results.

♦ One model that includes weekly support group meetings and involvement in community service activities has been implemented in several cities throughout the United States and has documented reductions in school dropout rates and pregnancy rates among enrolled teenagers. [254]

♦ Other service organization programs have not been evaluated adequately, although one reports differences between participants and controls that suggest that the program is effective in reducing pregnancy rates. [255]

♦ Recruitment into extracurricular prevention programs is often difficult, especially for those program components in which both the teenager and a parent are expected to participate. [256]

The value of these programs should not be discounted, however. By providing alternative role models for disadvantaged youth and involving them in community service projects, these programs can enhance adolescents' self-esteem and sense of the future, and may indirectly have some influence in lowering levels of teenage pregnancies and births.

Combining Education and Access to Contraceptive Services. Programs that combine sexuality education, counseling and small group discussions with easy access to medical family planning services have been successful in delaying the onset of sexual activity among participants, increasing contraceptive use rates among those who are sexually active and reducing pregnancy rates. [257]

It would appear that the success of this intensive approach depends, in part, on the rapport and trust that program staff, which often includes social workers and other professionals from external agencies, are able to establish with participants. Thus far, these intensive interventions have involved mainly high-risk youth in inner-city schools. [258]

Over the last decade, school-based and school-linked health clinics have become increasingly common. Over 400 such clinics are now in existence. [259]

♦ Many of these clinics provide sexuality education and reproductive health care and counseling, but only 33% dispense condoms or other methods of birth control. [260]

♦ Some studies of school-based clinics that provide comprehensive contraceptive services show significant declines in pregnancy rates and birthrates among students in those schools, but others demonstrate no significant reductions in these rates. [261]

Growing national concern over the threat of AIDS has led to the establishment of condom distribution programs in some public schools. Although such programs are now favored by 60% of adults, [262] only 8% of the nation's high school and middle school students live in districts where condom distribution programs have been approved. [263] To date, none of these programs has been evaluated to assess the impact on condom use or levels of STD transmission.

Organized family planning clinics are an important resource for teenagers who are sexually experienced and need medical contraceptive services.

♦ Nearly 30% of women who obtain services from family planning clinics are under age 20. [264]

Students do not appear to change their sexual behavior or increase their use of contraceptives unless the program provides specific information on how to resist sexual pressures and how to prevent pregnancy and disease.

Programs designed to increase teenagers' knowledge about sexuality and to improve access to contraceptive services do not encourage participants to engage in sexual activity.

♦ Teenagers often prefer to obtain services from clinics rather than from private physicians because of lower fees and a belief that clinics offer greater confidentiality.[265]

♦ Teenagers attending family planning clinics with special protocols for adolescents have relatively few problems with contraceptive use, high continuation rates and low pregnancy rates.[266]

Comprehensive, communitywide approaches that encourage abstinence by teaching communication and life skills, provide accurate information on contraceptive methods and STD prevention, and facilitate access to contraceptives have been implemented in a limited number of places. In some cases, such programs have been successful in reducing birthrates among adolescents. They are most likely to be successful if they have broadbased community support from parents, the schools, churches, community leaders and even the media. In one evaluated program, for example, teachers and school administrators attended graduate-level sex education courses at a local college, and clergy, community leaders and parents were recruited to attend comprehensive, one-day seminars. Schools were then better equipped to integrate family life education into the curriculum at all grade levels (K–12), while lay people and community leaders were trained to be better parents and role models for teenagers.[267] Staff at the schools also arranged for sexually experienced students to have access to contraceptive services in the community and distributed condoms on-site. However, a reevaluation of this program found that while community teenage birthrates declined significantly during the program's first three years, they returned to preintervention levels once the program lost its momentum and school personnel were restrained in their efforts to facilitate contraceptive access.[268]

Many communities around the country have formed coalitions aimed at developing strategies to reduce teenagers' levels of unintended pregnancies and likelihood of engaging in risk-taking behaviors. These coalitions have obtained commitments from community officials and funding agencies and have begun to initiate a variety of activities, including media campaigns, school programs, outreach activities, referrals and case coordination. Originally, evaluation was not included as a component of any of these efforts, but several communities have subsequently used available funds to develop comprehensive approaches, encompassing systematic evaluations of both the processes involved and the outcomes measured. None of these evaluations has yet been completed or published, however.[269]

Abstinence as the Only Choice. Some programs take a very narrow approach to adolescent sexuality: They promote abstinence until marriage as the only moral and healthy choice for teenagers and explicitly refuse to provide information about contraceptive methods or STD prevention.

♦ In the short run, students who go through such a program report more favorable opinions regarding abstinence than do those who have not received such instruction.[270]

♦ No scientific evaluations have demonstrated that such curricula actually raise the likelihood that students will abstain from sexual activity.

♦ Once they become sexually active, teenagers who have participated in one of these programs may be at higher risk for pregnancy and STDs because they have less information, as well as less-accurate information, about prevention strategies, and may even be misinformed about the use and effectiveness of specific methods.[271]

Sexual Activity Not Encouraged. An important finding of many evaluations of primary prevention efforts is that programs designed to increase teenagers' knowledge about sexuality issues, including pregnancy and STD prevention, and to improve access to medical contraceptive services do not encourage participants to engage in sexual activity earlier or more frequently than their peers who are not involved in such programs; nor do they result in higher pregnancy rates or birthrates in the communities where they are located.[272]

This finding is valid even though several national surveys of young people conducted in the 1970s and early 1980s produced inconsistent conclusions regarding the relationship between sex education and the initiation of sexual activity.

♦ Two studies suggested that young people aged 15–17, but not 18–19-year-olds, are more likely to initiate intercourse if they have taken a sex education course.[273]

♦ Other national studies have found either that there is no relationship between sex education and the initiation of sexual activity, or that teenagers who receive sex education are less likely than others to be sexually active.[274]

Among all of these studies, data on the content and comprehensiveness of the sex education received are lacking. Thus, conclusions regarding the association between sex education and sexual activity based on past national surveys are less reliable than are conclusions based on studies that evaluate the effects of specific educational curricula using quasi-experimental procedures to assign students into intervention and control groups.

In fact, while some of the evaluated programs show no significant impact on adolescent sexual activity, others show that participation lowers teenagers' likelihood of initiating sexual activity.

♦ For example, compared with controls, 6–38% fewer teenagers who participated in three evaluated programs were sexually active at the time of the evaluation follow-up.[275]

♦ Typically, the programs documenting the largest differences between participants and controls in terms of sexual activity and contraceptive use are the most intensive, ongoing programs, combining several approaches in an attempt to reach high-risk youth.

Programs for Pregnant Teenagers and Adolescent Parents

Many programs focus on improving teenagers' access to clinical reproductive health services, whether in school-based, school-linked or family planning clinics. These programs facilitate early detection of pregnancy among adolescents, and allow young women to consider all possible options for resolving their pregnancy, including adoption and abortion.

So far, there are few data on the effects of programs that focus primarily on providing teenagers with information about adoption and encouraging this option, although several studies have compared either the prior characteristics or the later outcomes of teenagers who choose to relinquish through adoption a baby whose birth was unintended with those of adolescent parents who choose to raise the child themselves.[276] As noted earlier, however, few teenage mothers place their infants for adoption, and the proportion who do so has been declining.[277]

Federal law stipulates that pregnant students may not be barred from attending schools that receive public funds.[278] Intensive, school-based programs have been implemented to deal with a variety of needs unique to the relatively small group of teenagers who become parents. These programs include services that help teenagers finish high school (especially child care) and facilitate career planning, and have resulted in more teenagers' remaining in school after the birth of their child.[279]

♦ In some cases, these programs are integrated with regular school courses, and the young women are offered special courses stressing the importance of prenatal care and teaching infant care and skills needed for parenthood. Day care may be provided, and caseworkers may meet with pregnant teenagers to assess and coordinate other services they may need, such as prenatal care, welfare benefits, counseling and child care.

♦ In other cases, these programs are separate from the regular school program, and participants attend all courses apart from other students during their pregnancies and usually for a short time postpartum.

Private and publicly funded group homes and residential care centers are available in some communities and large cities for a small number of young women who can no longer remain at home. These homes may offer pregnant teenagers and adolescent parents a place to live where they can receive social and financial support, child care and counseling while they complete high school or get job training.

The most intensive programs use a case management approach to facilitate medical and social support for teenagers during pregnancy and after the birth of their child. These programs have some-

AT EACH SUCCESSIVE REPRODUCTIVE STAGE, FEWER, AND INCREASINGLY DISADVANTAGED, TEENAGERS...

Although most teenage women do not proceed from one reproductive stage to the next...

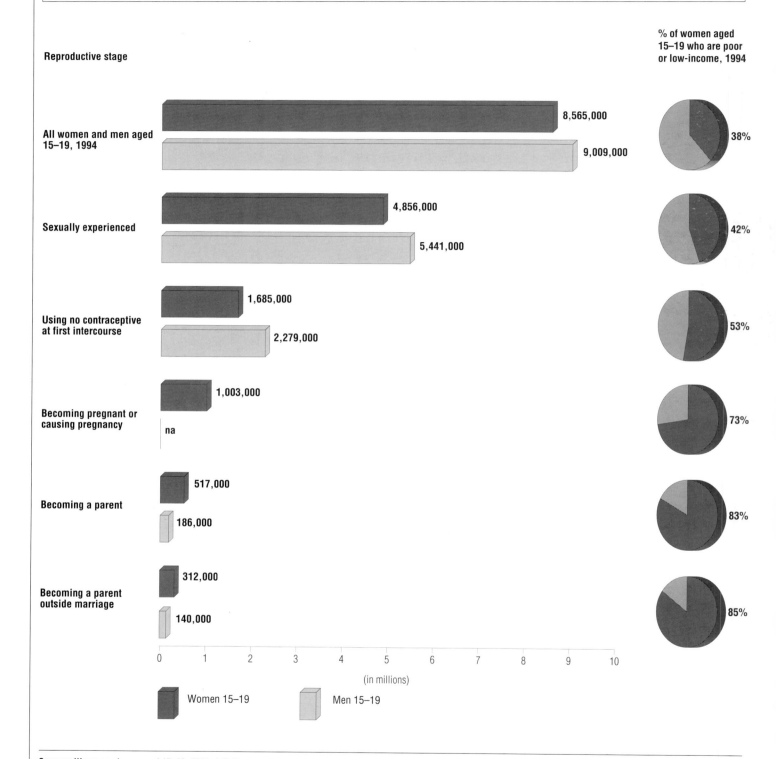

Reproductive stage

% of women aged 15–19 who are poor or low-income, 1994

All women and men aged 15–19, 1994
8,565,000
9,009,000
38%

Sexually experienced
4,856,000
5,441,000
42%

Using no contraceptive at first intercourse
1,685,000
2,279,000
53%

Becoming pregnant or causing pregnancy
1,003,000
na
73%

Becoming a parent
517,000
186,000
83%

Becoming a parent outside marriage
312,000
140,000
85%

0 1 2 3 4 5 6 7 8 9 10
(in millions)

■ Women 15–19   □ Men 15–19

Sources: Women and men aged 15–19, 1994: J. C. Day, "Population Projections of the United States, by Age, Sex, Race, and Hispanic Origin: 1992 to 2050," *Current Population Reports*, Series P-25, No. 1092, 1992, Table 2, p. 16. **Women sexually experienced** and **women using no**

contraceptive at first intercourse: AGI tabulations of data from the 1988 National Survey of Family Growth. **Men sexually experienced** and **men using no contraceptive at first intercourse:** F. L. Sonenstein, J. H. Pleck, and L. C. Ku, "Sexual Activity, Condom Use and AIDS Awareness Among

Adolescent Males," *Family Planning Perspectives*, **21**: 152–158, 1989, Tables 1 and 5, pp. 153 and 155. **Women becoming pregnant:** S. K. Henshaw, "U.S. Teenage Pregnancy Statistics," AGI, New York, 1993. **Women and men becoming parents (total and outside marriage):**

FIGURE 54

...AND VERY DIFFERENT INTERVENTION SERVICES NEEDED

...those who do are likely to be already disadvantaged and to need more intensive intervention services.

Sexuality education · Contraceptive services · Outreach · Options counseling · Abortion services · Prenatal care · Adoption counseling · School completion programs · Child care · Parental skills · Programs to become economically self-sufficient · Welfare and Medicaid · Child support

AGI tabulations of data from the 1988 National Maternal and Infant Health Survey; tabulations of data from the 1987 AGI Abortion Patient Survey. **% of women who are poor or low-income, 1994:** AGI tabulations of data from the March 1992 Current Population Survey.

Notes: na: not available; the number of men aged 15–19 causing pregnancy cannot be calculated because data on the age of men involved in pregnancies ending in abortion are not available. **Data for 1994:** Estimated by applying the most recently available gender-specific and, for women, poverty

status–specific, proportions of persons at each reproductive stage to the projected number of persons aged 15–19 of that gender in 1994. This assumes that trends will remain constant from the year the proportions were derived.

> **The intensity of the interventions required depends on where along the reproductive spectrum teenagers are.**

times resulted in increased levels of prenatal care among teenagers, a decline in the number of low-birth-weight infants, fewer repeat pregnancies among teenage mothers, higher graduation rates and greater economic self-sufficiency.[280] Some of these positive effects last only a short time, however.[281] In the longer run, differences between program participants and controls in terms of repeat pregnancies and graduation rates diminish, which indicates that these programs are most effective in crisis management and that strategies to deal with the long-term consequences of teenage parenthood are still needed. Community-based or clinic-based programs that encourage adolescent mothers to use contraceptives and to refrain from having further nonmarital births in their teenage years also lead to declines in repeat pregnancies, at least in the short term.[282]

A policy of offering increased welfare payments to teenage parents as an incentive to remain in school, and of reducing welfare payments for those who drop out, has been found to increase school attendance by teenage parents. The results are preliminary, however, and it is not clear whether such a policy causes graduation rates to go up.[283]

It is relatively easy to increase teenagers' knowledge about sexuality, but getting them to change their behavior requires more intensive interventions. The intensity of the interventions required depends on where along the reproductive spectrum teenagers are. For example, all teenagers need information and interpersonal skills; sexually active teenagers need access to contraceptive services. Adolescents who become parents require much more intensive interventions—ones that go far beyond even the most comprehensive sex education program and that include programs to help them stay in school, child care services and instruction in parenthood skills. Many also need programs to help young parents become economically self-sufficient, welfare and Medicaid, and child support payments from the baby's father if the parents are not married or living together (Figure 54, pages 70–71).

Where Do We Go from Here?

Adolescent sexuality is a complex issue with trends and counter-trends that make it difficult for policymakers, parents and others to know how to respond. Even the facts often appear in doubt or contradictory. Periodically, the media trumpet reports that adolescent pregnancy rates are "soaring," and indeed, rates among all adolescent women have gone up as sexual activity has become more common in the teenage years. At the same time, pregnancy rates among sexually experienced teenagers—who, after all, are the young women at risk of getting pregnant—have declined significantly since the early 1970s. Birthrates among sexually experienced adolescents have also declined (despite a slight rise recently) during this time.

An accurate appraisal of the situation is complicated by the fact that the outcomes of sex among teenagers that are clearly negative—STDs, unintended pregnancy, abortion and too-early childbearing—are intertwined with such profoundly difficult issues as poverty, race, family structure and substance abuse. Thus, it becomes easy and tempting, for some, to dismiss early sexual activity as a phenomenon confined to teenagers in poor, inner-city areas and dysfunctional families, or as part of a hopeless tangle of social pathology.

This report shows the reality to be quite different. The transition to adulthood has been radically, and probably irrevocably, altered by major social changes. Marriage and childbearing now generally occur much later, and initiation of sexual intercourse much earlier, than they did several decades ago. Most adolescents, regardless of their race, income status, gender or religious affiliation, begin to have sex in their middle to late teens. We must deal with these facts, even if we do not like them.

And we are not alone in our quandary. Current trends in sexual behavior are hardly unique to U.S. teenagers. They mirror trends among U.S. adults, as well as teenage and adult women and men around the world. In the last 20 years, for example, the proportion of births to U.S. women in their early 20s that were out of wedlock quadrupled.[284] Indeed, it is adult women, not teenagers, who account for most unintended pregnancies, abortions and nonmarital births every year. Out-of-wedlock childbearing has also become more common worldwide, and the increase has been less dramatic in the United States than in some other developed countries, including Australia, Austria, New Zealand and Norway.[285]

So, where do we go from here? What can we—as individuals, as parents, and as a society—do to help young people avoid the negative, at times life-altering, effects of sexual activity?

When, If Ever, Are Teenagers Ready for Sex?

This is one of the most troubling questions for adults—and frequently for young people as well. The issue is difficult because there is no defining moment or event—as marriage was for earlier generations—that marks the point at which a person is considered ready for sex, or at least the point at which it is considered appropriate to have sex. Often, teenagers are simply told to wait until they are "older." Age alone, however, is no guarantee of readiness for sex, or for the assumption of many other adult responsibilities, for that matter.

For people who believe that sex outside marriage is morally wrong, the answer to the question of timing, presumably, is that unmarried people—adults as well as teenagers—should not have sexual intercourse. While this view may run counter to current trends, it is entitled to respect and support. Most adults, however, are more concerned that their children avoid the negative consequences of sex if they do begin to have intercourse. Their views on the appropriateness of teenage sex are undoubtedly affected by the maturity of the individuals involved.

Most adults are troubled by the thought of very young teenagers' having sex, which, in fact, is relatively rare. Still, there are a number of reasons why young teenagers should be encouraged to delay the initiation of sexual intercourse: Sex among young adolescents is often involuntary; it frequently involves a man who is

An accurate appraisal of the situation is complicated by the fact that the negative outcomes of sex among teenagers are intertwined with such profoundly difficult issues as poverty, race, family structure and substance abuse.

substantially older than the woman, which may make it hard for the young woman to resist his approaches and even more difficult for her to insist that contraceptives be used to prevent STDs and pregnancy; teenagers who have intercourse at a young age tend to have relatively unstable relationships and to quickly acquire other sexual partners, which increases their risk of exposure to an STD; and biologically, young teenagers are the most susceptible to a sexually transmitted infection. Additionally, young teenagers who get pregnant are rarely, if ever, in a position to support and raise a family.

For older adolescents, it may be more appropriate—and more effective—to stress the importance of postponing sex until they are sufficiently mature to treat their partner with respect and to assume responsibility for protecting themselves and their partner from the negative consequences of sex. At a minimum, this would mean that they would not consider having intercourse until they are responsible enough to use contraceptives correctly and consistently to prevent an unintended pregnancy and the transmission of an STD.

What If Teenagers Become Sexually Active?

While we should do all we can to delay the initiation of intercourse among adolescents until they achieve a certain level of maturity, there is no clear dividing line that can be established for all young people. Furthermore, some teenagers will ignore admonitions. Many will consider themselves "ready" to have sex whether we agree or not. Thus, it is imperative that we give all adolescents, whatever their age or level of maturity, the knowledge, the means and, perhaps most important of all, strong encouragement to take the necessary steps to protect themselves from the life-altering risks of pregnancy and disease.

And they can do that. Even now, a large majority of teenagers who have sex use contraceptives to prevent pregnancy and STDs, even the first time they have intercourse. Indeed, it cannot be stressed often enough that adolescents generally use contraceptives at least as effectively as adults.

Why Do Teenagers Get Pregnant or Contract an STD?

Sexually experienced teenagers, like adult women and men, do get pregnant accidentally and acquire sexually transmitted infections. Some 3 million teenagers each year acquire an STD, which can have serious, long-term health ramifications, and more than 1 million adolescent women become pregnant, the vast majority of them unintentionally.

Teenagers tend to delay use of the most effective methods of contraception for a substantial period of time after their first act of intercourse, and like older couples, they sometimes use contraceptives incorrectly and sporadically. They also face the same dilemma: whether to choose a method, such as the condom, that protects against STDs and pregnancy, but has a relatively high failure rate in actual use, or to depend on a method, such as the pill, that offers greater protection against pregnancy and does not need the cooperation of one's partner, but provides no protection against sexually transmitted infections.

Teenagers, moreover, face a host of difficulties that do not confront adult women: lack of experience in negotiating with their partner about contraceptive use; fear of disclosure; lack of access to a source of appropriate care; and the barrage of contradictory messages about contraception and responsible behavior emanating from the media, schools, their peers and sometimes their parents.

Teenage Childbearing: Are There Two Tracks?

When adolescent women become pregnant unintentionally, the path they follow in resolving their dilemma is determined largely by their income and socioeconomic status. Young women from advantaged families generally have abortions, so they can finish their education, get a good job and establish their financial independence before they have children. Poor and low-income teenagers also frequently have abortions; more often, however, they continue their pregnancies to term and raise the children themselves. It bears repeating that more than 80% of teenagers who give birth are poor or of marginal income.

Childbearing among unwed teenagers is often cited as the cause of some of the country's most difficult problems—poverty, welfare dependence, crime, drug abuse and homelessness. About a quarter of young women who have a child as a teenager are poor later in their lives, but their poverty is as much a function of their initial economic, social and educational disadvantage as it is of becoming a teenage parent. Policymakers and others who want to reform the nation's welfare system by, among other things, denying eligibility to unwed mothers[286] should understand that while this change might cut the welfare rolls, it would not address a major underlying cause of adolescent childbearing—namely, poverty. Furthermore, such a drastic step might reinforce adverse effects of poverty for subsequent generations of children.

Few would disagree that it would be better for everyone involved, as well as for society in general, if every child were born into a two-parent family. That, in fact, is the aspiration of most teenagers, whatever their actual life circumstances. Surveys show that adolescents overwhelmingly want to marry and to raise their children with a spouse.[287] All too often, however, the young women who have births in their teenage years are unable to make that aspiration a reality. These young people know that they can have a better life if they get a good education that leads to a decent job, but if they cannot, or think they cannot, achieve these goals, they have little incentive to postpone childbearing. The reality is that many, if not most, of the young women who become adolescent mothers face restricted options for the future, poor prospects for finding decent jobs and little chance of marriage.

What Interventions Are Needed?

No single approach to adolescent sexuality and its consequences is appropriate for all teenagers of all ages in all circumstances and in every community. Nevertheless, it is clear that all teenagers need certain interventions if they are to avoid the negative consequences of sex. All adolescents, for example, need sex education that teaches them the interpersonal skills they will need to withstand pressure to have sex until they are ready, and that includes accurate, up-to-date information about

methods to prevent pregnancy and STDs—and they need this before they begin to have sex.

But education and knowledge are not enough. Teenagers also need clear, strong messages, coming first from their parents and reinforced by the schools, the media and other sources, about the importance of making conscious decisions about whether to have intercourse; about the necessity of consistent, correct condom use to protect themselves and their partners from HIV and other STDs; and about the use of condoms or another method of contraception to prevent unintended pregnancies. Additionally, all sexually experienced teenagers, including young men, need easy access to contraceptive services and STD screening and treatment. The network of freestanding, publicly supported family planning clinics that is a major provider of confidential family planning and STD services for teenagers, especially young women, has been weakened in recent years by serious underfunding. Moreover, its future is uncertain in the face of health care reform efforts. Teenagers' access to these confidential services must be maintained and expanded, whether through a discrete clinic system or through broader health care networks.

Teenagers of all income levels also need access to abortion services. Young women who are poor or low-income are substantially less likely than their more advantaged peers to terminate their pregnancies. Surely, one reason for the difference is that most state Medicaid programs will not pay for abortions for indigent women except in very limited circumstances (but will pay for services related to childbirth). Congress took a first, but largely symbolic, step toward the restoration of Medicaid coverage when it voted, in the fall of 1993, to allow payment for abortions needed by women whose pregnancies resulted from rape or incest.[288] It must go further, however, and extend coverage to all abortions, so that women of all income levels have the same opportunity to terminate a pregnancy if they conclude that they are not in a position to bear and raise a child. Additionally, abortion must be included on the list of basic services in whatever health care reform package is ultimately

In most other industrialized societies, there is greater openness about sexual relationships; the media provide positive reinforcement for using contraceptives to avoid pregnancy and STDs; and reproductive health care is better integrated into general health services.

AN INTERNATIONAL PERSPECTIVE ON TEENAGE PREGNANCY

The United States, compared with many other industrialized countries, has high adolescent pregnancy rates.

Pregnancies per 1,000 women aged 15–19 and younger, 1988

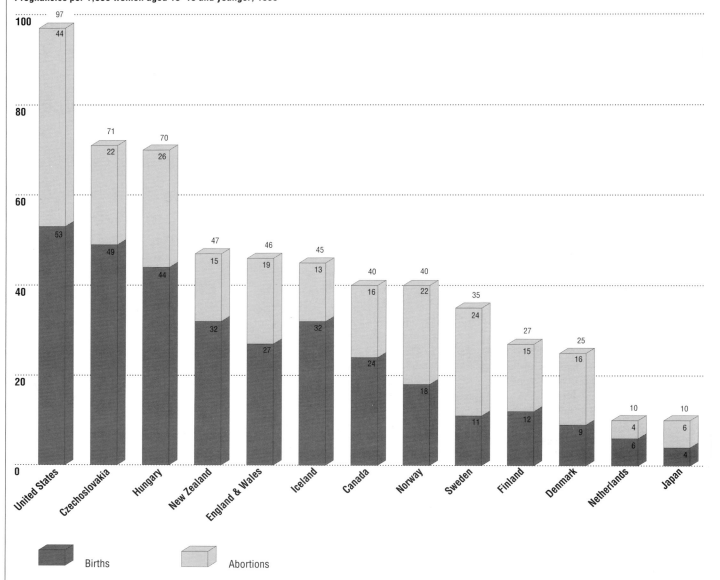

Births   Abortions

Sources: United States: Birthrate—National Center for Health Statistics, "Advance Report of Final Natality Statistics, 1988," *Monthly Vital Statistics Report*, Vol. 39, No. 4, Supplement, 1990, Table 3. **Abortion rate**—S. K. Henshaw, "Abortion Trends in 1987 and 1988: Age and Race," *Family Planning Perspectives,* 24:85–86, 1992, Table 1, p. 69.

Czechoslovakia: Number of births—United Nations, *Demographic Yearbook, 1990,* New York, 1992, Table 11, p. 335. **Number of abortions**—Vydava Ustav zdravotnickych inofmaci a statistiky, *Zdravotnicka Statistika CSSR, Potraty, 1988,* Prague, 1989, Table 64, p. 35. **Total women 15–19**—Population data for women aged 15–19 were interpolated from United Nations, *Demographic Yearbook, 1987,* New York, 1989, Table 7, p. 246; United Nations, *Demographic Yearbook, 1989,* New York, 1991, Table 7, p. 190.

Hungary: Birthrate—Council of Europe, *Recent Demographic Developments in Europe, 1991,* Strasbourg, 1991, Table H-3, p. 119. **Abortion rate**—Ferenc Kauraras, "In Your Part of the World: Survey of Central and Eastern Europe (Part I)," *Entre Nous,* No. 14–15, 1990, pp. 13–14, Table 1, p. 14.

New Zealand: Birthrate—United Nations, *Demographic Yearbook, 1990,* New York, 1992, Table 11, p. 336. **Number of abortions**—Abortion Supervisory Committee to Parliament, "Report of the Abortion Supervisory Committee, for the Year Ended 31 March 1990," Wellington, New Zealand, Table 2, p. 4. **Total women 15–19**—Interpolated from United Nations, *Demographic Yearbook, 1989,* New York, 1991, Table 7, p. 198; United Nations, *Demographic Yearbook, 1987,* New York, 1989, Table 7, p. 246.

England and Wales: Number of births—Office of Population Censuses and Surveys, "Birth Statistics, 1988," London, 1990, Table 3.1, p. 28. **Number of abortions**—Office of Population Censuses and Surveys, *Abortion Statistics, 1988,* Series AB, No. 15, London, 1989, Table 3, p. 6. **Total women 15–19**—Office of Population Censuses and Surveys, *Key Population of Vital Statistics,* London, 1990, Table A1, p. 83.

Iceland, Norway, Sweden, Finland and Denmark: Birthrates and abortion rates—Nordic Medico-Statistical Committee, *Health Statistics in the Nordic Countries, 1966–1991,* Copenhagen, 1991, Table 5.a, p. 121.

Canada: Birthrate—Statistics Canada, *Selected Birth and Fertility Statistics, Canada, 1921–1990,* Ottawa, 1993, Table 10, p. 46. **Abortion rate**—Statistics Canada, "Therapeutic

FIGURE 55

adopted. Better sex education and improved access to contraceptive, STD and abortion services will not be sufficient, however, to address the root cause of early childbearing among disadvantaged teenage women who become parents. For these young women, entrenched poverty, not adolescent pregnancy, is the fundamental problem that must be addressed. Some will have the grit, the inborn talent and, somehow, the support to escape their circumstances. But for most, real change in sexual behavior and its outcomes will become likely only when their poverty is alleviated, when they—and their partners—have access to good schools and jobs, and when they develop a sense that their life can get "better."

Change Is Possible

The United States is not alone in grappling with the implications of adolescent sexual activity or unwed motherhood. However, teenage pregnancy, abortion and childbearing are larger problems in this country than in many other developed nations (Figure 55, page 76)—even though levels of adolescent sexual activity are about the same. In most other industrialized societies, there is greater openness about sexual relationships; the media provide positive reinforcement for using contraceptives to avoid pregnancy and STDs; and reproductive health care is better integrated into general health services, which make contraceptives more accessible to teenagers.[289]

Sources, Figure 55, continued

Abortions, 1988," *Health Reports*, **2**(1), Supplement, Ottawa, 1990, Table 6, p. 25.

Netherlands: Birthrate—Council of Europe, *Recent Demographic Developments in Europe, 1991*, Strasbourg, 1991, Table NL, p. 158. **Number of abortions**—J. Rademakers, *Abortus in Nederland 1987–1988*, Stimezo-Onderzoek, Utrecht, 1990, Tables 2.1 and 2.2, pp. 8 and 10. **Total women 15–19**—United Nations, *Demographic Yearbook, 1989*, New York, 1991, Table 7, p. 192.

Japan: Birthrate—United Nations, *Demographic Yearbook, 1989*, New York, 1991, p. 321, Table 11. **Abortion rate**—Kuno Kitamura, "Every Child Should Be a Wanted Child," *Integration*, Dec. 1991, Table 2, p. 42. **Total women 15–19**—United Nations, *Demographic Yearbook, 1989*, New York, 1991, Table 7, p. 184.

Note: Pregnancies are the sum of births and abortions and do not include miscarriages. For New Zealand and Japan, the numerator is births and abortions among all women aged 19 and younger. In all other cases, the numerator is births and abortions among women aged 15–19. The denominator is women aged 15–19.

In the United States, by contrast, sex education is still controversial in some communities; the full panoply of contraceptives is often not readily accessible to teenagers (or to many adults, for that matter); and the media are reluctant to discuss or portray responsible sexual behavior, preferring to offer a mindless and constant display of titillating sexuality. Indeed, nothing better illustrates this country's unwillingness to confront sexual issues directly than its failure to use the national media, particularly the national television networks, to educate young people and adults alike about the importance of using protection against pregnancy and STDs, including AIDS, an invariably fatal disease. Incredibly, although the networks have agreed to run public service announcements about the importance of using condoms to prevent HIV and other STD transmission, they still refuse to accept advertising for the very same products for the purpose of preventing pregnancy, on the ground that it would offend some viewers. Americans seem to prefer bemoaning the high rates of adolescent pregnancy, abortion and childbearing to taking positive steps to address those issues. In many respects, it seems, it is adults, not teenagers, who act irresponsibly.

In an effort to develop more effective policies for helping American youth, there is much to be learned from the approaches of countries where teenagers are much less likely to experience negative outcomes of sexual behavior. We can also learn from the handful of programs, described in the previous section of this report, that have had a positive impact on teenagers' initiation of sexual intercourse and contraceptive use. These programs need to be adapted to local circumstances and widely replicated. In addition, other approaches must be tested and implemented in a variety of school systems and communities.

Many young people are managing the transition to adulthood well: They are succeeding in school, building healthy relationships with friends of both sexes, avoiding STDs and unintended pregnancy when they become sexually active, and preparing for careers. Often, however, they accomplish some of these tasks without appreciable guidance and support

Nothing better illustrates this country's unwillingness to confront sexual issues than its failure to use the national media to educate young people and adults about the importance of using protection.

from their parents and other adults (who tend to be uncomfortable talking about sex with children), schools and other institutions. In most other aspects of life, society tries to ensure that young people have the information and skills they will need to function as competent adults. We try to give them a good education, provide job skills, instill values and establish standards of behavior. When it comes to sex, however, we say little or nothing and expect that upon reaching a magical age, young people will know how to manage such an important part of their lives. We know that avoidance is not working, not only for young women and men, but also for adults, who even more than teenagers experience the negative consequences of sex. So, we are paying a high price for our silence in two ways: First, many of our children are—needlessly—affected adversely by the consequences of their sexual behavior. Second, today's teenagers become tomorrow's adults, and the problems they had as teenagers do not go away, but are perpetuated into adulthood and passed on to the next generation.

We can and must do better. ◆◆◆◆

Notes to Text

1. Nathanson, 1991, pp. 59–72.

2. Saluter, 1992, Figure 2, p. 4; Table C, p. 5.

3. Greeley, Michael and Smith, 1989, p. 25.

4. Reiss, 1991, p. 7; Moore and Steif, 1989, pp. 6–7.

5. McKinney and Peak, 1994; Leitman, Kramer and Taylor, 1993.

6. Lapham and del Pinal, 1993, Table 1, p. 4.

7. Bezilla, 1988, pp. 132–133.
Those surveyed were between the ages of 13 and 17.

8. Federer, 1991.

9. Bezilla, 1988, pp. 34–35.

10. Crimmins, Easterlin and Saito, 1991, Table 8, p. 127.

11. George H. Gallup International Institute, 1992.

12. Opinion Research Corp., 1993, Questions T6 and T11.
Some 60% of 12–17-year-olds cite AIDS as the reason for teenagers not to have sex, while 25% mention pregnancy. Only 8% say they think premarital sex is morally wrong. Young teenagers are more likely than older teenagers to cite fear of AIDS as a reason not to have sex and are less likely to mention the risk of pregnancy.

13. Hollmann, 1993, Table 1, p. 2.

14. AGI, 1993a.

15. Wilson, 1987, pp. 20–62.

16. AGI, 1993a.

17. Wilson, 1987, pp. 100–104.

18. AGI, 1993b.

19. AGI, 1993b.

20. Marini, 1989, p. 344; Lester, 1990.

21. Thomson, McLanahan and Curtin, 1992, Table 3, p. 373.

22. Morrison and Cherlin, 1992; Wu and Martinson, 1993, p. 228.

23. AGI, 1993b; Billy et al., 1993, Table 1, p. 54.

24. Trent and South, 1992, p. 438.

25. Federer, 1991; U.S. Bureau of the Census, 1992, Table 299, p. 186.
In 1988, 29% of black households and 24% of white households were victims of crime.

26. Bezilla, 1988, pp. 54–55, 192–193.

27. U.S. Bureau of the Census, 1992, Table 300, p. 186.

28. Chadwick and Heaton, 1992, Table H1-20, p. 250; Randall, 1992, p. 3127.

29. NCHS, 1991, Table 1-26, pp. 246–305.
About 16,000 young people aged 15–19 die annually. Some 49% die in accidents, 19% are murdered, 13% commit suicide, 6% die from disease, and 14% die of natural causes.

30. Hardy, 1992.

31. Moss et al., 1992.
Heavy smoking is defined as having at least five cigarettes a day for at least 10 days a month.

32. CDC, 1991a, Table 2, p. 661.
Heavy drinking is defined as having at least five alcoholic drinks on at least one occasion within a 30-day period.

33. CDC, 1991a, Table 2, p. 661; AGI, 1993c.

34. Institute for Health Policy, 1993, p. 22.

35. Dryfoos, 1990.

36. AGI, 1993a.

37. Osterman, 1980.

38. Steinberg, 1982, pp. 196–197.

39. AGI, 1993a.

40. At the same time, the cost of a college education has increased considerably. In constant dollars, between 1979–1980 and 1989–1990, the annual cost for a public college increased 31%, to $4,978, and the cost for a private college rose 51%, to $12,349. (Federer, 1991.)

41. Kominski and Adams, 1992, Table 9, pp. 59–60.
Among year-round, full-time workers aged 18–24, the median income for high school graduates in 1990 was $13,300 for women and $15,300 for men. The median income for college graduates was $20,300 for women and $22,800 for men.

42. U.S. Bureau of the Census, 1992, Table 64, p. 52.

43. Louis Harris and Associates, 1988; Stipp, 1993.
On average, 12–17-year-olds watch about 24 hours of television a week. Seven of these hours are during prime time, when, on average, network shows include 28 references to or depictions of sexual behavior per hour. In contrast, there is less than one reference per hour to contraception, abortion, STDs or sexuality education.

44. Harris/Scholastic Research, 1993, pp. 7–11, 13.
Overall, 81% of students (85% of young women and 76% of young men) have been exposed to unwelcome sexual comments or actions, ranging from comments or gestures to being forced into some type of sexual behavior other than kissing (11% of all students, 13% of young women and 9% of young men).

45. Bezilla, 1988, p. 201.

46. AGI, 1993b; AGI, 1993h.

47. Opinion Research Corp., 1993, Question T2.
About two-thirds of teenagers aged 12–17 (72% of young men and 63% of young women) first learn about sex from someone other than their parents: 24% from friends; 23% from school; and 17% from the media.

48. Bezilla, 1988, pp. 15, 42.
Among teenagers aged 13–15 and those aged 16–17, 28% would like to talk more about sex with their parents. Some 44% of 13–15-year-olds and 36% of 16–17-year-olds think parents provide the most accurate information. Some 25% of each age-group think they get the most accurate information from their friends, while 24% of 13–15-year-olds and 17% of 16–17-year-olds think teachers are the most accurate source of information.

49. AGI, 1993b.

50. AGI, 1993b.

51. AGI, 1993b.

52. Forrest and Silverman, 1989, Figure 1, p. 69; AGI, 1993b; AGI 1993h.

53. CDC, 1991b.
Among people aged 18 and older surveyed in 1989, 25% thought the average American has intercourse before age 14, and 62% thought first intercourse typically occurs before age 16

54. Forrest, 1993; Sonenstein, Pleck and Ku, 1989; U.S. Bureau of the Census, 1989.

55. AGI, 1993b; AGI, 1993c; Hollmann, 1993, Table 1, p. 10; Sonenstein, Pleck and Ku, 1989, Table 1, p. 153.

56. AGI, 1993b; Hofferth, 1986; Tanfer, 1993.

57. U.S. Bureau of the Census, 1991, Table A, p. 1.

58. AGI, 1993a.

59. AGI, 1993a.

60. Axinn and Thornton, 1993, p. 233; Bumpass and Sweet, 1989, Table 3, p. 619.

61. AGI, 1993b.

62. AGI, 1993b.

63. Forrest, 1993, Table 2, p. 107; Table 4, p. 109.

64. Forrest, 1993, Tables 4 and 5, p. 109.
On average, white and Hispanic women wait about six years; white and Hispanic men wait just over nine years.

65. Saluter, 1992, Table 1, p. 9; Wilson, 1987, pp. 63–92.
Fewer than half of black women and men have married by age 25–29, compared with about six in 10 white and Hispanic men and more than seven in 10 women. In part, the low marriage rates among blacks reflect the poor job prospects for young black men.

66. AGI, 1993b; Hofferth, 1986; Hofferth, Kahn and Baldwin, 1987, Table 3, p. 49.

67. Forrest and Singh, 1990; AGI, 1993b.

68. Sonenstein, Pleck and Ku, 1989, Table 2, p. 154.

69. Udry and Billy, 1987, pp. 846–849.

70. Smith, 1988.
Some teenagers' responses to survey questions about sexual behavior may be affected by pressures they feel to cover up facts or by a sense that they are expected to be sexually active. Thus, some of the differences— such as high levels of sexual activity among young black men and low levels among Hispanic, white and higher income women—may reflect not only real differences in behavior, but also differences in what these groups feel is socially desirable or acceptable to tell someone else, especially an adult female interviewer.

71. Forrest, 1993, Table 3, p. 107; Table 4, p. 109.

72. Forrest, 1993.

73. AGI, 1993c.

74. AGI, 1991.

75. Adapted by AGI from Moore, Nord and Peterson, 1993.
According to these rates, if no young teenagers were forced to have sex involuntarily, the proportion of 15-year-old women who have had intercourse would decline 35%.

76. Moore, Nord and Peterson, 1989, p. 111.

77. Cassese, 1993; Kidman, 1993; Paone and Chavkin, 1993; Zierler et al., 1991.

78. Bezilla, 1988, pp. 14–15.
Pressure to have sex was less common in 1988 than in 1982, when 31% of 13–17-year-olds reported feeling pressure to engage in sexual relationships, or in 1985, when 29% did so. Even so, young people today are more likely to have felt pressure to have sex than to smoke (23%). Those aged 16–17 are more likely to have felt pressure to have sex (29%) than are younger teenagers, but even 13–15-year-olds have felt pressured (23%). Some 28% of women and 23% of men have felt pressured to have sex.

79. AGI, 1993b.
Teenagers are more likely than older women to have more than one sexual partner in a given period only when they are compared with *all* older women, including those who are married.

80. Kost and Forrest, 1992, p. 247.

81. Kost and Forrest, 1992, pp. 246–248; Sonenstein, Pleck and Ku, 1991, p. 163.
Never-married, sexually experienced men aged 15–19 in 1988 reported an average of five sexual partners, while sexually experienced women in that age-group reported an average of three partners (AGI, 1993b).

82. AGI, 1993b.

83. AGI, 1993b.

84. Léridon, 1977.

85. Harlap, Kost and Forrest, 1991, p. 36.

86. Mosher, 1982, p. 24.

87. Atwater, 1992, pp. 61, 64; Bongaarts and Potter, 1983.

88. Donovan, 1993, pp. 18–24; Harlap, Kost and Forrest, 1991, pp. 42–44.

89. AGI, 1993b; Kost and Forrest, 1992, p. 248, Table 3.

90. Kost and Forrest, 1992, Table 5, p. 250; Figure 1, p. 247.

91. Moscicki et al., 1989; Ostergard, 1977, p. 59; Shafer and Sweet, 1990.

92. Shafer and Sweet, 1990, p. 550.

93. Polyurethane condoms may be at least as effective as latex condoms, although a final determination must await further study.

94. Kestelman and Trussell, 1991; Roper, Peterson and Curran, 1990; Saracco et al., 1993, p. 500.
Young men aged 15–19 are more likely to use condoms consistently if they are concerned about preventing pregnancy, are worried about getting AIDS or think their partners would appreciate condom use. They are less likely to use condoms if they are embarrassed or concerned about condoms' reducing sexual pleasure. (Pleck, Sonenstein, and Ku, 1991.)

95. See Figure 25 for the steps entailed in "perfect" condom use.

96. Cates and Stone, 1992a; Cates and Stone, 1992b.

97. Cates and Stone, 1992b, Table 7, p. 125.

98. Cassell, 1984.

99. AGI, 1993d.

100. Ku, Sonenstein and Pleck, 1993.

101. The pill must be taken daily; the injectable provides protection for three months; and the implant lasts for five years.

102. Harlap, Kost and Forrest, 1991, pp. 45–48.

103. Grady et al., 1993, p. 67; Table 2, p. 70.
Overall, 27% of men aged 20–39 say they are embarrassed buying condoms.

104. Levenson, Morrow and Pfefferbaum, 1984.

105. The Food and Drug Administration (FDA) has lifted its recommendation that a woman always have a pelvic examination before her initial prescription for oral contraceptives. Following the FDA's action, Title X family planning clinics were notified by the government that the examination may be deferred if a clinician determines that the woman has no indications of medical risk and has been counseled about the need to use protection against STD transmission. (Bennett, 1993.)

106. Forrest, Gold and Kenney, 1989, p. 36.

107. Chamie et al., 1982; Cheng et al., 1993.

108. Dryfoos, 1988, p. 198.

109. Henshaw and Torres, 1994.
Women under age 18 are not charged or are charged at a reduced rate for their initial visit in about 54% of family planning clinics and can get pills without charge or at a reduced rate at 62% of these clinics. When publicly funded clinics do not reduce fees, a routine first visit averages $50, and pills cost an average of $7 per cycle.

Contraceptive implants are generally available to those who can pay the full cost, including the cost of insertion, which typically runs about $500 in a family planning clinic (Frost, 1994, Table 5, pp. 9–10). They are also available to low-income, unmarried mothers who qualify for welfare and therefore are eligible for Medicaid. Teenage daughters in families covered by Medicaid can have their service fees covered by Medicaid.

110. Chapin, 1993.

111. Silverman and Torres, 1987, Table 25, pp. 145–147.
Some 54% of clinics, but only 32% of private doctors, see clients in the evening; 29% and 13%, respectively, have weekend hours. Some 31% of clinics will see women for routine care without an appointment, compared with only 15% of private physicians. Only 8% of clinics will refuse to serve a woman who cannot pay, compared with 38% of physicians. The average wait for an appointment at a clinic or private physician's office is 6–7 days.

112. Daley and Gold, 1993, p. 248.

113. Henshaw and Torres, 1994.

114. McKinney and Peak, 1994.

115. Leitman, Kramer and Taylor, 1993.

116. Forrest and Singh, 1990; Sonenstein, Pleck and Ku, 1989.

117. AGI, 1993b; Sonenstein, Pleck and Ku, 1989, p. 154.

118. Forrest and Singh, 1990, Table 5, p. 209; Hollmann, 1993, Table 1, p. 10; Sonenstein, Pleck, and Ku, 1989, Table 5, p. 155.

119. AGI, 1993b; Sonenstein, Pleck and Ku, 1989.
In 1988, for example, 77% of adolescent women who had been 18–19 at first intercourse reported that they or their partner had used a method at that time, compared with 68% of those who had first had sex between the ages of 15 and 17, and 52% of those who had begun intercourse before age 15.

120. Forrest and Singh, 1990, Table 5, p. 209; Sonenstein, Pleck and Ku, 1989, Table 5, p. 155.
Some 69% of white women and 66% of white men aged 15–19 in 1988 had used a method at first intercourse, compared with 49–57% of black and Hispanic men and women. Similarly, 73% of teenage women from higher income families had used a method at first intercourse, compared with 58% of poor and low-income teenagers.

121. Forrest and Singh, 1990, Table 5, p. 209.

122. Forrest and Singh, 1990, Table 5, p. 209.

123. AGI, 1993b.

124. AGI, 1993b.
Some 37% of black teenagers make a visit within three months, compared with 20% of Hispanic and white teenagers. Among women from poor families, 27% make a visit within three months, compared with 19% and 23%, respectively, of low-income and higher income teens.

125. AGI, 1993b.
Overall, 42% of women aged 18–19 at first intercourse visit a clinic or doctor for family planning within three months of starting intercourse, compared with 23% of those aged 15–17 and 18% of those under age 15.

126. AGI, 1993b.
Of those who first have sex before age 15, 74% go to a clinic for medical family planning services, compared with 68% of women aged 15–17 and 58% of those aged 18–19.

127. Forrest and Singh, 1990, p. 211.

128. AGI, 1993b.

129. Kost and Forrest, 1992, pp. 252, 253.

130. Oakley, 1993.

131. Jones and Forrest, 1992, p. 13; Table 3, p. 16.
When these data were obtained, the contraceptive implant and the injection were not available, and rates for the IUD could not be calculated.

132. Emans et al., 1987; Jones and Forrest, 1992, Table 2, p. 15.

133. Jones and Forrest, 1992, Table 2, p. 15.

134. CDC, 1993.
Some individuals are infected with more than one STD at the same time, but there are no data on the overlap of infections. In fact, all figures on the incidence and prevalence of STDs are rough. The Centers for Disease Control and Prevention, and this report, assumes that the number of infections equals the number of infected people.

135. Calculated by AGI on the basis of data in CDC, 1993a; Forrest and Singh, 1990; Harlap, Kost and Forrest, 1991; Sonenstein, Pleck and Ku, 1989; U.S. Bureau of the Census, 1990.

136. CDC, 1993; U.S. Bureau of the Census, 1990.

137. CDC, 1993, p. 29; Donovan, 1993.

138. Effler et al., 1992; Schachter, 1989, p. 803.

139. Moscicki et al., 1990, p. 507.

140. CDC, 1993, Figure 17.

141. CDC 1992, Figure 21; Forrest and Singh, 1990, Table 3, p. 208; Billy et al., 1993 Table 1, p. 54; Sonenstein, Pleck and Ku, 1989, Table 1, p. 153.

142. CDC, 1993, Table 19, p. 207.
Screening of military recruits indicates that three teenagers in 10,000 entering the military are infected with HIV; the rate among black teenagers is one in 1,000. Screening of youth aged 16–21 entering the Job Corps, a program that provides education, job training and employment to disadvantaged teenagers, finds a higher level of HIV infection—about four per 1,000. Entrants who are black have the highest infection rate—five per 1,000, compared with three per 1,000 for Hispanics and one per 1,000 for white youth. On average, the incubation period between infection and onset of AIDS is 11 years.

143. Aral and Guinan, 1984; Donovan, 1993.

144. CDC, 1993; Donovan, 1993, pp. 24–25; Harlap, Kost and Forrest, 1991, pp. 42–44.

145. Forrest and Cates, 1993; Harlap, Kost and Forrest, 1991, pp. 45–55.

146. Harlap, Kost and Forrest, 1991, pp. 53–55.

147. Harlap, Kost and Forrest, 1991, p. 55; Kestelman and Trussell, 1991, pp. 226–227.

148. Harlap, Kost and Forrest, 1991, pp. 50–52.

149. Wasserheit, 1992, pp. 61–77.

150. AGI, 1993b; Henshaw, Koonin, and Smith, 1991, Table 4, p. 78; Hollmann, 1993.
In addition, each year, some 20-year-olds who conceived when they were 19 have abortions, miscarriages or births (approximately 185,000 in 1990). In this report, pregnancies are classified by the woman's age at the time of the birth, abortion or miscarriage, not by her age at the time of conception.

151. Henshaw, 1993.
Pregnancies among women under 15 account for fewer than 3 percent of all pregnancies among teenagers. Between 1987 and 1990, the pregnancy rate increased less than 1% for all women under 14, rose 5% for 15–17 year-old women, and climbed 8% for women aged 18–19 and 20–24 .

152. Henshaw, 1993.
Rates among sexually experienced women aged 15–17 were lower in 1990 than in any previous year for which data were collected; they were lower for 18–19-year-old women for all years except 1987, 1988 and 1989.

153. Henshaw, 1993.
Overall, 62% of teenage pregnancies in 1990 occurred among women aged 18–19, compared with 58% in 1972. Between 1972 and 1990, the number of pregnancies among women under age 15 remained between 28,000 and 32,000; the number among 15–17-year-olds declined from 389,000 to 363,000, while the number among older teenagers increased from 561,000 to 649,000.

154. AGI, 1993b; Henshaw, 1993.
The proportion of women who become pregnant is much smaller among younger teenagers than among older adolescents. Fewer than 2% of all 14-year-olds become pregnant each year, compared with 7% of 15–17-year-olds, 17% of those aged 18–19 and 20% of 20–24-year-olds.

155. AGI, 1993b.
Every year, 32% of sexually experienced black teenage women, compared with 26% of Hispanics and 15% of whites, become pregnant.

156. NCHS, 1990b, Table 1-10, pp. 1–14.

157. AGI, 1993d; AGI, 1993e; Henshaw, 1992, Table 1, p. 86.

158. AGI, 1993d; AGI, 1993e; Henshaw, 1992, Table 1, p. 86; Hollmann, 1993; Sonenstein, Pleck and Ku, 1989, Table 1, p. 153.

159. Forrest, 1993, p. 108.

160. AGI, 1993b.
Because of differences in how young women resolve their pregnancies, the median gap between conception and first birth is almost five years among white women, compared with only three years among blacks and two years among Hispanics.

161. AGI, 1993d; Henshaw, 1992, Table 1, p. 86.
Only women aged 25–34 have more intended pregnancies than unintended ones. Pregnancies ending in miscarriage are excluded from the calculations.

162. AGI, 1993d; Henshaw, 1992, Table 1, p. 86.
Pregnancies ending in miscarriage are excluded from the calculations.

163. AGI, 1993d; AGI 1993e; Henshaw, 1992, Table 1, p. 86.
Among pregnant women 15–19 in 1988, 93% of higher income teenagers had gotten pregnant accidentally, compared with 83% of poor teenagers and 79% of low-income adolescents. By contrast, 35% of pregnancies among higher income women aged 25–29 were unintended, compared with 72% and 53%, respectively, among poor and low-income women in that age-group.

164. AGI, 1993d; AGI, 1993e; Henshaw, 1992, Table 1, p. 86.
Of the 135,000 annual intended pregnancies among women under age 20, 21% are among blacks and 19% are among Hispanic teenagers. In contrast, blacks account for 29% of all unintended teenage pregnancies, but Hispanics account for only 13%.

165. AGI, 1993d; AGI 1993e; Henshaw, 1992, Table 1, p. 86.

166. Henshaw and Van Vort, 1989, p. 85.

167. Henshaw, 1992, Table 1, p. 86.

168. AGI, 1993d; Henshaw, 1992.

169. AGI, 1993d; AGI, 1993e; Henshaw, 1992, Table 1, p. 86.

170. Zabin, Hirsch and Boscia, 1990, pp. 109, 112.

171. AGI, 1993d; AGI, 1993e; Henshaw, 1992, Table 1, p. 86.

172. AGI, 1993d; AGI, 1993e; Henshaw, 1992, Table 1, p. 86

173. Daley and Gold, 1993, p. 244; Table 2, pp. 250–251.

174. Henshaw, 1991, p. 249.

175. Cooksey, 1990, p. 213.

176. Blum and Resnick, 1982.

177. AGI, 1993d; AGI, 1993e; Henshaw, 1992, Table 1, p. 86.

178. AGI, 1993d; AGI, 1993e; Henshaw, 1992, Table 1, p. 86.

179. Torres and Forrest, 1988, Table 1, p. 170.

180. Donovan, 1992, pp. 6–7, 10–11; Appendix Table 1, pp. 30–35.
The age of majority is 19 in Alabama, Nebraska and Wyoming. In Mississippi, it is 21, although the general age of consent to medical care is 18.

More than half the states have laws that expressly permit minors to obtain prenatal care and delivery services on their own consent, and nearly half authorize minors to consent to contraceptive services. All states except South Carolina explicitly allow minors to obtain STD testing and treatment without their parents' knowledge. South Carolina, however, authorizes minors 16 and older to consent to any legal health service.

181. Donovan, 1992, pp. 23–26.

182. Henshaw and Kost, 1992, p. 199; Table 3, p. 200; Table 5, p. 202.

183. Henshaw and Kost, 1992, Table 8, pp. 205–206.
Nine in 10 of these young women consult their boyfriend; nearly a quarter talk with a professional, such as a health care provider or minister or rabbi; half consult another adult.

184. Bachrach, Stolley and London, 1992, Table 1, p. 29; Figure 1, p. 31.

185. NCHS, 1993b, Table 4, p. 20.

Between the mid-1960s and mid-1980s, the annual birthrate averaged only one birth per 1,000 women under age 15 and about 34 per 1,000 for women aged 15–17. Among 18–19-year olds and 20–24-year-olds, birthrates declined sharply from 1966 through 1976 and remained relatively stable for the next 10 years at about 80 per 1,000 and 111 per 1,000, respectively. Between 1986 and 1991, the birthrate steadily increased, from about 31 per 1,000 to 39 per 1,000 for 15–17-year-olds, and from about 80 per 1,000 to 94 per 1,000 for 18–19-year-olds.

186. Moore, 1993, p. 2.

187. NCHS, 1993b, Table 2, p. 18.

188. AGI, 1993d; NCHS, 1990a, Table 2, p. 16.

189. AGI, 1993d.

190. NCHS, 1993a, Table 3, p. 20; Table 24, p. 40; Table 25, p. 41.

191. NCHS, 1993a, Table 24, p. 40.

192. Moore, 1993.

193. Bachu, 1991, Table E, p. 7.

194. NCHS, 1993a, Table 2, pp. 18–19; Table 16, p. 33.

195. AGI, 1993d.

196. AGI, 1993b.
More than four in 10 black brides have a child, compared with fewer than one in 10 Hispanic and white brides. Older teenagers are about twice as likely as younger brides to already have a child when they marry, but women under age 18 are more likely to be pregnant.

197. AGI, 1993b.

198. AGI, 1993b; AGI, 1993d.

199. AGI, 1993b.

200. AGI, 1993d.

201. AGI, 1993b.

202. AGI, 1993b.

203. AGI, 1993b.

204. AGI, 1993f.
Public assistance includes Aid to Families with Dependent Children (AFDC), general assistance, food stamps and emergency assistance.

205. Furstenberg, Brooks-Gunn and Morgan, 1987a, p. 145.

206. AGI, 1993f.

207. Center for Population Options, 1992, Table 1, p. 5.

208. Lester, 1990, Table A, p. 2; Table C, p. 5; Table D, p. 6.

209. AGI, 1993d.
Among 16-year-old women giving birth, 25% have a male partner who is younger than 17, and 53% have a partner younger than 20. Black mothers under age 18 are most likely to have a teenage partner; 59% do so, compared with 48% and 36%, respectively, of young white and Hispanic mothers.

210. NCHS, 1967, Table 1-48, pp. 1–57, 1-58; NCHS, 1993a, Table 2, pp. 18–19.
Between 1965 and 1990, the proportion of first births that were to teenagers declined about 40% (from 35% to 21%) among whites and 29% (from 59% to 42%) among blacks.

211. AGI, 1993b.

212. Upchurch and McCarthy, 1990, pp. 226–228.

213. Furstenberg, Brooks-Gunn and Morgan 1987a, p. 143.

214. Upchurch and McCarthy, 1990, Figure 2, p. 227; pp. 228, 231.

215. Kalmuss and Namerow, 1992, p. 12.

216. Polit and Kahn, 1986, pp. 168–170, and Table 4, p. 170; Kalmuss and Namerow, 1992, p. 21.

217. Hofferth and Hayes, 1987, Table 8.2, p. A-144.

218. AGI, 1993b; Martin and Bumpass, 1989, Tables 1 and 2, pp. 41 and 42.

219. Hofferth, 1987, pp. 134–135.

220. Hoffman, 1993; Hoffman, Foster and Furstenberg, 1993.

221. Makinson, 1985, p. 134.

222. Makinson, 1985.

223. Singh, Forrest and Torres, 1989, Table 2.2, p. 20.

224. AGI, 1993d.
Some 15% of 15–17-year-old pregnant women and 11% of 18–19-year-olds either receive no prenatal care (3% of each age-group) or begin care only in the third trimester.

225. AGI, 1993d.
Among 15–17-year olds, 16% of blacks and 14% of whites and Hispanics receive no prenatal care before the third trimester. Among 18–19-year-olds, 15% of blacks, 14% of Hispanics and 7% of whites go without prenatal care that long.

226. AGI, 1993d.
Some 18% of teenager mothers whose family income prior to their pregnancies was at least $25,000 a year receive prenatal care only in the third trimester or not at all, compared with 12% of young women whose family income was below $12,000.

227. NCHS, 1993b, pp. 7–8; Table 13, p. 28.
In 1991, 8% of infants born to white teenagers and 13% of those born to blacks were underweight.

228. Hayes, 1987, pp. 124–125, 196–200; Hofferth and Hayes, 1987, pp. 116, 176–177.

229. AGI, 1993d.
Some 23% of babies born to black women aged 15–17 are premature, compared with 19% of babies born to Hispanics in that age-group and 9% of babies born to whites.

230. AGI, 1993g.

231. Bumpass, 1990, p. 485.

232. AGI, 1993g.

233. AGI, 1993g.

234. Hofferth and Hayes, 1987, pp. 181–199.

235. Furstenberg, Brooks-Gunn and Morgan, 1987a; Furstenberg, Brooks-Gunn and Morgan, 1987b.

236. See, e.g., Howard and McCabe, 1992.

237. Gambrell and Kantor, 1992/1993.

238. Dryfoos, 1990.

239. Kirby et al., 1993, p. 14.

240. Henshaw and Van Vort, 1990, p. 105.

241. AGI, 1993b.

242. Ku, Sonenstein and Pleck, 1992, Table 1, p. 102.

243. AGI, 1993b; Ku, Sonenstein and Pleck, 1992, Table 1, p. 102.

244. Britton, De Mauro and Gambrell, 1992/1993, p. 2; Haffner, 1992, p. 1.

245. Kenney, Guardado and Brown, 1989, p. 56.

246. Kirby, 1984, pp. 385–407.

247. Kirby 1984, pp. 385–407; Kirby et al., 1994; Stout and Rivara, 1989.

248. Anderson et al., 1990, p. 252; Ku, Sonenstein and Pleck, 1992, p. 100; Walter and Vaughn, 1993, pp. 725, 728.

249. Barth et al., 1992; Eisen and Zellman, 1992; Howard and McCabe, 1992; Walter and Vaughn, 1993, p. 725.

250. Zabin, 1992, p. 170.

251. Barth et al., 1992, p. 70; Howard and McCabe, 1990, p. 24; Zabin, 1992, p. 173.

252. See, e.g., Walter and Vaughn, 1993, Figure 54, p. 728.

253. Kirby et al., 1994.

254. Philliber and Allen, 1992.

255. Nicholson and Postrado, 1992.

256. Brindis, 1991; Nicholson and Postrado, 1992, pp. 124–125.

257. Zabin et al., 1986.

258. Zabin et al., 1986, Figure 1, p. 122; Zabin, 1992, p. 158.

259. McKinney and Peak, 1994.

260. McKinney and Peak, 1994.

261. Dryfoos, 1988, p. 196; Edwards et al., 1980, p. 6; Kirby et al., 1993, p. 12; Kirby and Waszak, 1992, p. 211; Zabin, 1992.

262. Elam, Rose and Gallup, 1993, pp. 15–16.

263. Leitman, Kramer and Taylor, 1993, p. 4.

264. CDC, 1994, pp. 31–34.

265. Chamie et al., 1982, p. 137.

266. Ralph and Edgington, 1983, p. 158; Winter and Breckenmaker, 1991, p. 24.

267. Vincent, Clearie and Schluchter, 1987.

268. U.S. Congress, Office of Technology Assessment, 1991, pp. 368–371.

269. Brindis, 1991, ch. 3, pp. 47–76.

270. Olsen et al., 1991, pp. 639–640.

271. Trudell and Whatley, 1991, p. 125.

272. Berger et al., 1987, p. 436; Dryfoos, 1988, pp. 193–196; Forrest, Hermalin and Henshaw, 1981, pp. 112–113; Kirby et al., 1994; Kirby and Waszak, 1992, p. 211.

273. Marsiglio and Mott, 1986, p. 151; Zelnik and Kim, 1982, p. 123.

274. Dawson, 1986, p. 162; Furstenberg, Moore and Peterson, 1985, p. 1331; Ku, Sonenstein and Pleck, 1992, pp. 102–103.

275. Barth et al., 1992, p. 69; Howard and McCabe, 1992, p. 102; Zabin et al., 1986, p. 122.

276. Bachrach, Stolley and London, 1992; Kalmuss, Namerow and Cushman, 1992; McLaughlin, Manninen and Winges, 1988.

277. Bachrach, Stolley and London, 1992, p. 29, Table 1.

278. Title IX of the Educational Amendments of 1972.

279. Wallace, Weeks and Medina, 1982; Warrick et al., 1993; Zellman, 1982.

280. Korenbrot et al., 1989, p. 97; Polit, 1989, p. 164; Rabin, Seltzer and Pollack, 1992, p. 66.

281. Hanson, 1992; Polit, 1989, p. 165.

282. Kates, 1990, pp. 10–11.

283. Bloom et al., 1991, p. 155.

284. Moore, 1993, Table, p. 2.

285. Ferguson, 1993, Table 2, p. 639.

286. Murray, 1993.

287. Bezilla, 1988, p. 35; Crimmins, Easterlin and Saito, 1991, Table 1, p. 119.

288. P.L. 103-112 (Oct. 21, 1993).

289. Jones et al., 1986.

References

Alan Guttmacher Institute (AGI), "Politics of Sex Halts Youth Survey," *Family Planning Perspectives*, 23:197, 1991.

AGI, tabulations of data from the March 1992 Current Population Survey, 1993a.

AGI, tabulations of data from the 1988 National Survey of Family Growth, 1993b.

AGI, tabulations of data from the 1990 Youth Risk Behavior Survey, 1993c.

AGI, tabulations of data from the 1988 National Maternal and Infant Health Survey, 1993d.

AGI, tabulations of data from the 1987 AGI Abortion Patient Survey, 1993e.

AGI, tabulations of data from the 1987 National Survey of Families and Households, 1993f.

AGI, tabulations of data from the 1988 National Health Interview Survey—Child Supplement, 1993g.

AGI, tabulations of data from the 1988 National Survey of Adolescent Males, 1993h.

Anderson, E., *Street Wise*, University of Chicago Press, Chicago, 1990.

Anderson, J. et al., "HIV/AIDS Knowledge and Sexual Behavior Among High School Students," *Family Planning Perspectives*, 22:252–255, 1990.

Aral, S. O. and M. E. Guinan, "Women and Sexually Transmitted Diseases," in K. K. Holmes et al., eds., *Sexually Transmitted Diseases*, McGraw-Hill, New York, 1984, pp. 85–89.

Atwater, E., *Adolescence*, third ed., Prentice-Hall, Englewood Cliffs, N.J., 1992.

Axinn, W. G. and A. Thornton, "Mothers, Children, and Cohabitation: The Intergenerational Effects of Attitudes and Behavior," *American Sociological Review*, 58:233–246, 1993.

Bachrach, C. A., K. S. Stolley and K. A. London, "Relinquishment of Premarital Births: Evidence from National Survey Data," *Family Planning Perspectives*, 24:27–32, 1992.

Bachu, A., "Fertility of American Women: June 1990," *Current Population Reports*, Series P-20, No. 454, 1991.

Barth, R. P. et al., "Enhancing Social and Cognitive Skills," in B. C. Miller et al., eds., *Preventing Adolescent Pregnancy*, Sage Publications, Newbury Park, Calif., 1992, pp. 53–82.

Bennett, J., Acting Deputy Assistant Secretary for Population Affairs, Memorandum to Regional Health Administrators, Washington, D.C., June 25, 1993.

Berger, D. K. et al., "Influence of Family Planning Counseling in an Adolescent Clinic on Sexual Activity and Contraceptive Use," *Journal of Adolescent Health Care*, 8:436–440, 1987.

Bezilla, R., ed., *America's Youth 1977–1988*, The Gallup Organization, Princeton, 1988.

Billy, J. O. G. et al. "The Sexual Behavior of Men in the United States," *Family Planning Perspectives*, 25:52–60, 1993.

Blum, R. W. and M. D. Resnick, "Adolescent Sexual Decision-Making: Contraception, Pregnancy, Abortion, Motherhood," *Pediatric Annals*, 11:797–805, 1982.

Bloom, D. et al., *LEAP: Implementing a Welfare Initiative to Improve School Attendance Among Teenage Parents*, Manpower Demonstration Research Corporation, New York, 1991.

Bongaarts, J. and R. Potter, *Biology and Behavior:*

An Analysis of the Proximate Determinants, Academic Press, New York, 1983.

Brindis, C. D., *Adolescent Pregnancy Prevention*, Health Promotion Resource Center, Stanford Center for Research in Disease Prevention, Palo Alto, Calif., 1991.

Britton, P. O., D. De Maruo and A. E. Gambrell, "HIV/AIDS Education: SIECUS Study on HIV/AIDS Education for Schools Finds States Make Progress, but Work Remains," *SIECUS Report*, 21(2):1–8, 1992/1993.

Bumpass, L. L., "What's Happening to the Family? Interactions Between Demographic and Institutional Change," *Demography*, 27:483–498, 1990.

Bumpass, L. L. and J. A. Sweet, "National Estimates of Cohabitation," *Demography*, 26:615–625, 1989.

Cassell, C., *Swept Away*, Simon & Schuster, New York, 1984.

Cassese, J., "The Invisible Bridge: Child Abuse and the Risk of HIV Infection in Childhood," *SIECUS Report*, 21(4):1–7, 1993.

Cates Jr., W. and K. M. Stone, "Family Planning, Sexually Transmitted Diseases and Contraceptive Choice: A Literature Update—Part I," *Family Planning Perspectives*, 24:75–84, 1992a.

Cates Jr., W. and K. M. Stone, "Family Planning, Sexually Transmitted Diseases and Contraceptive Choice: A Literature Update—Part II," *Family Planning Perspectives*, 24:122–128, 1992b.

Center for Population Options, *Teenage Pregnancy and Too-Early Childbearing: Public Costs, Personal Consequences*, Washington, D.C., 1992.

Centers for Disease Control and Prevention (CDC), "Current Tobacco, Alcohol, Marijuana and Cocaine Use Among High School Students—United States, 1990," *Morbidity and Mortality Weekly Report*, 40:659–663, 1991a.

CDC, "Perceptions About Sexual Behavior: Findings from a National Sex Knowledge Survey—United States, 1989," *Morbidity and Mortality Weekly Report*, 40:255–259, 1991b.

CDC, *Division of STD/HIV Prevention 1991 Annual Report*, Atlanta, 1992.

CDC, *Division of STD/HIV Prevention 1992 Annual Report*, Atlanta, 1993.

CDC, "Characteristics of Women Receiving Family Planning Services at Title X Clinics—United States, 1991," *Morbidity and Mortality Weekly Report*, 43:31–34, 1994.

Chadwick, B. A. and T. B. Heaton, eds., *Statistical Handbook of the American Family*, Oryx Press, Phoenix, 1992.

Chamie, M. et al., "Factors Affecting Adolescents' Use of Family Planning Clinics," *Family Planning Perspectives*, 14:126–139, 1982.

Chapin, J., American College of Obstetricians and Gynecologists, personal communication, June 23, 1993.

Cheng, T. L. et al., "Confidentiality in Health Care: A Survey of Knowledge, Perceptions, and Attitudes Among High School Students," *Journal of the American Medical Association*, 269:1404–1407, 1993.

Cooksey, E. C. "Factors in the Resolution of Adolescent Premarital Pregnancies," *Demography*, 27:207–218, 1990.

Crimmins, E. M., R. A. Easterlin and Y. Saito, "Preference Changes Among American Youth: Family, Work, and Goods Aspirations, 1976–85," *Population and Development Review*, 17:115–133, 1991.

Daley, D. and R. B. Gold, "Public Funding for Contraceptive, Sterilization and Abortion Services, Fiscal Year 1992," *Family Planning Perspectives*, 25:244–251, 1993.

Dawson, D. A., "The Effects of Sex Education on Sexual Behavior," *Family Planning Perspectives*, 18:162–170, 1986.

Donovan, P., *Our Daughters' Decisions: The Conflict in State Law on Abortion and Other Issues*, AGI, New York, 1992.

Donovan, P., *Testing Positive: Sexually Transmitted Disease and the Public Health Response*, AGI, New York, 1993.

Dryfoos, J. G., "School-Based Health Clinics: Three Years of Experience," *Family Planning Perspectives*, 20:193–200, 1988.

Dryfoos, J. G., *Adolescents-at-Risk: Prevalence and Prevention*, Oxford University Press, New York, 1990.

Edwards, L. E. et al., "Adolescent Pregnancy Prevention Services in High School Clinics," *Family Planning Perspectives*, 12:6–14, 1980.

Effler, P. et al., "High Prevalence of Chlamydia in Female Adolescents Reporting Only One Lifetime Sex Partner," paper presented at the 32nd Interscience Conference on Antimicrobial Agents and Chemotherapy, Anaheim, Calif., Oct. 11–14, 1992.

Eisen, M. and G. L. Zellman, "A Health Benefits Field Experiment: Teen Talk," in B. C. Miller et al., eds., *Preventing Adolescent Pregnancy*, Sage Publications, Newbury Park, Calif., 1992, pp. 220–264.

Elam, S. M., L. C. Rose and A. M. Gallup, 25th Annual Gallup/Phi Delta Kappa Poll of the Public's Attitudes Toward the Public Schools, conducted for Phi Delta Kappa International, Bloomington, Ind., Oct. 1993.

Emans, S. J. et al., "Adolescents' Compliance with the Use of Oral Contraceptives," *Journal of the American Medical Association*, 257:3377–3381, 1987.

Federer, L., *Youth Indicators, 1991. Trends in the Well-Being of American Youth*, Office of Educational Research and Improvement, Washington, D.C., 1991.

Ferguson, J., "Youth at the Threshold of the 21st Century: The Demographic Situation," *Journal of Adolescent Health*, 14:638–644, 1993.

Food and Drug Administration, Fertility and Maternal Health Drug Advisory Committee vote, Washington, D.C., May 20, 1993.

Forrest, J. D., "Timing of Reproductive Life Stages," *Obstetrics and Gynecology*, 82:105–111, 1993.

Forrest, J. D. "Thirtysomething and Beyond," paper presented at the Center for Population Research, National Institute of Child Health and Human Development and The Rockefeller Foundation Conference on Opportunities in Contraception: Research and Development, Bethesda, Md., February 1992.

Forrest, J. D., R. B. Gold and A. M. Kenney, *The Need, Availability and Financing of Reproductive Health Services*, AGI, New York, 1989.

Forrest, J. D., A. I. Hermalin and S. K. Henshaw, "The Impact of Family Planning Clinic Programs on Adolescent Pregnancy," *Family Planning Perspectives*, 13:109–116, 1981.

Forrest, J. D. and J. Silverman, "What Public School Teachers Teach About Preventing Pregnancy, AIDS and Sexually Transmitted Diseases," *Family Planning Perspectives*, 21:65–72, 1989.

Forrest, J. D. and S. Singh, "The Sexual and Reproductive Behavior of American Women, 1982–1988," *Family Planning Perspectives*, 22:206–214, 1990.

Frost, J. J., "The Availability and Accessibility of the Contraceptive Implant from Family Planning

Agencies in the United States, 1991–1992," *Family Planning Perspectives*, 26:4–10, 1994.

Furstenberg Jr., F. F., J. Brooks-Gunn and S. P. Morgan, "Adolescent Mothers and Their Children in Later Life," *Family Planning Perspectives*, 19:142–151, 1987a.

Furstenberg Jr., F. F., J. Brooks-Gunn and S. P. Morgan, *Adolescent Mothers in Later Life*, Cambridge University Press, New York, 1987b.

Furstenberg Jr., F. F., K. Moore and J. Peterson, "Sex Education and Sexual Experience Among Adolescents," *American Journal of Public Health*, 75:1331–1332, 1985.

Gambrell, A. E. and L. M. Kantor, "The Far Right and Fear-Based Abstinence-Only Programs," *SIECUS Report*, 21(2):16–18, 1992/1993.

George H. Gallup International Institute, *The Religious Life of Young Americans: A Compendium of Surveys on the Spiritual Beliefs and Practices of Teen-agers and Young Adults*, Princeton, 1992.

Grady, W. R. et al., "Condom Characteristics: The Perceptions and Preferences of Men in the United States," *Family Planning Perspectives*, 25:67–73, 1993.

Greeley, A. M., R. T. Michael and T. W. Smith. "A Most Monogamous People: Americans and Their Sexual Partners," National Opinion Research Center, Chicago, 1989.

Haffner, D. W., "1992 Report Card on the States: Sexual Rights in America," *SIECUS Report*, 20(3):1–7, 1992.

Hanson, S. L., "Involving Families in Programs for Pregnant Teens: Consequences for Teens and Their Families," *Family Relations*, 41:303–311, 1992.

Hardy, J., Johns Hopkins University School of Medicine, personal communication, May 19, 1992.

Harlap, S., K. Kost and J. D. Forrest, *Preventing Pregnancy, Protecting Health: A New Look at Birth Control Choices in the United States*, AGI, New York, 1991.

Harris/Scholastic Research, *Hostile Hallways: The AAUW Survey on Sexual Harassment in America's Schools*, American Association of University Women Educational Foundation, Washington, D.C., 1993.

Hayes, Cheryl D., ed., *Risking the Future: Adolescent Sexuality, Pregnancy and Childbearing, Vol. I*, National Academy Press, Washington, D.C., 1987.

Henshaw, S. K., "The Accessibility of Abortion Services in the United States," *Family Planning Perspectives*, 23:246–252, 263, 1991.

Henshaw, S. K. "Abortion Trends in 1987 and 1988: Age and Race," *Family Planning Perspectives*, 24:85–86, 1992.

Henshaw, S. K., "U.S. Teenage Pregnancy Statistics," AGI, New York, 1993.

Henshaw, S. K., L. M. Koonin and J. C. Smith, "Characteristics of U.S. Women Having Abortions, 1987," *Family Planning Perspectives*, 23:75–81, 1991.

Henshaw, S. K. and K. Kost, "Parental Involvement in Minors' Abortions Decisions," *Family Planning Perspectives*, 24:196–207, 213, 1992.

Henshaw, S. K. and A. Torres, "Family Planning Agencies: Services, Policies and Funding," *Family Planning Perspectives*, 26:52–59, 82, 1994.

Henshaw, S. K. and J. Van Vort, "Teenage Abortion, Birth and Pregnancy Statistics: An Update," *Family Planning Perspectives*, 21:85–88, 1989.

Henshaw, S. K. and J. Van Vort, "Abortion Services in the United States, 1987 and 1988," *Family Planning Perspectives*, 22:102–108, 1990.

Hofferth, S. L., tabulations of data from the 1982 National Survey of Family Growth, 1986.

Hofferth, S. L., "Social and Economic Consequences of Teenage Childbearing," in S. L. Hofferth and C. D. Hayes, eds., *Risking the Future: Adolescent Sexuality, Pregnancy, and Childbearing, Vol. II*, National Academy Press, Washington, D.C., 1987, pp. 123–144.

Hofferth, S. L. and C. D. Hayes, eds., *Risking the Future: Adolescent Sexuality, Pregnancy and Childbearing, Vol. II*, National Academy Press, Washington, D.C., 1987.

Hofferth, S. L., J. R. Kahn and W. Baldwin, "Premarital Sexual Activity Among U.S. Teenage Women over the Past Three Decades," *Family Planning Perspectives*, 19:46–53, 1987.

Hoffman, S. D., tabulations of data from the 1987 Panel Study of Income Dynamics, 1993.

Hoffman, S. D., E. M. Foster and F. F. Furstenberg Jr., "Reevaluating the Costs of Teenage Childbearing," *Demography*, 30:1–13, 1993.

Hollmann, F. W., "Estimates of the Population of the United States by Age, Sex, and Race," U.S. Bureau of the Census, *Current Population Reports*, Series P-25, No. 1095, 1993.

Howard, M. and J. B. McCabe "Helping Teenagers Postpone Sexual Involvement," *Family Planning Perspectives*, 22:21–26, 1990.

Howard, M. and J. B. McCabe, "An Information and Skills Approach for Younger Teens: Postponing Sexual Involvement Program," in B. C. Miller et al., eds., *Preventing Adolescent Pregnancy*, Sage Publications, Newbury Park, Calif., 1992, pp. 83–109.

Institute for Health Policy, *Substance Abuse: The Nation's Number One Health Problem*, Brandeis University, Waltham, Mass., 1993.

Jones, E. F. et al., *Teenage Pregnancy in Industrialized Countries*, Yale University Press, New Haven and London, 1986.

Jones, E. F. and J. D. Forrest, "Contraceptive Failure Rates Based on the 1988 National Survey of Family Growth," *Family Planning Perspectives*, 24:12–19, 1992.

Kalmuss, D. S. and P. B. Namerow, "The Mediators of Educational Attainment Among Early Childbearers," paper presented at the National Institute of Child Health and Human Development Conference on the Outcomes of Early Childbearing, Bethesda, Md., May 18–19, 1992.

Kates, N., "Buying Time: The Dollar-a-Day Program," John F. Kennedy School of Government, Harvard University, Cambridge, Mass., 1990.

Kenney, A. M., S. Guardado and L. Brown, "Sex Education and AIDS Education in the Schools: What States and Large School Districts Are Doing," *Family Planning Perspectives*, 21:56–64, 1989.

Kestelman, P. and J. Trussell, "Efficacy of Simultaneous Use of Condoms and Spermicides," *Family Planning Perspectives*, 23:226–232, 1991.

Kidman, C., "Non-Consensual Sexual Experience & HIV Education: An Educator's View," *SIECUS Report*, 21(4):9–12, 1993.

Kirby, D., *Sexuality Education: An Evaluation of Programs and Their Effects*, Network, Santa Cruz, Calif., 1984.

Kirby, D. and C. Waszak, "School-Based Clinics," in B. C. Miller et al., eds., *Preventing Adolescent Pregnancy*, Sage Publications, Newbury Park, Calif. 1992, pp. 185–219.

Kirby, D. et al., "The Effects of School-Based Health Clinics in St. Paul on School-Wide Birthrates," *Family Planning Perspectives*, 25:12–16, 1993.

Kirby, D. et al., "School-Based Programs to Reduce Sexual Risk Behaviors: A Review of Effectiveness," *Public Health Reports*, 109:339–360, 1994.

Kominski, R. and A. Adams, "Educational Attainment in the United States: March 1991 and 1990," *Current Population Reports*, Series P-20, No. 462, 1992.

Korenbrot, C. C. et al., "Birth Weight Outcomes in a Teenage Pregnancy Case Management Project," *Journal of Adolescent Health Care*, 10:97–104, 1989.

Kost, K. and J. D. Forrest, "American Women's Sexual Behavior and Exposure to Risk of Sexually Transmitted Diseases," *Family Planning Perspectives*, 24:244–254, 1992.

Ku, L., F. L. Sonenstein and J. H. Pleck, "The Association of AIDS Education and Sex Education with Sexual Behavior and Condom Use Among Teenage Men," *Family Planning Perspectives*, 24:100–106, 1992.

Ku, L., F. L. Sonenstein and J. H. Pleck, "The Dynamics of Young Men's Condom Use During and Across Relationships," paper presented at the National Institute of Child, Health and Human Development Conference on Behavioral Research on the Role of Condoms in Reproductive Health, Bethesda, Md., May 10, 1993.

Lapham, S. and J. del Pinal, *Persons of Hispanic Origin in the United States, 1990*, U.S. Bureau of the Census, Population Division, Ethnic and Hispanic Statistics Branch, Washington, D.C., 1993.

Leitman, R., E. Kramer and H. Taylor, "A Survey of Condom Programs," in S. E. Samuels and M. D. Smith, eds., *Condoms in the Schools*, Henry J. Kaiser Family Foundation, Menlo Park, Calif., 1993.

Léridon, H., *Human Fertility: The Basic Components*, J. F. Helzner, trans., University of Chicago Press, Chicago, 1977.

Lester, G. H., "Child Support and Alimony: 1987," *Current Population Reports*, Series P-23, No. 167, 1990.

Levenson, P. M., J. R. Morrow Jr., and B. J. Pfefferbaum, "A Comparison of Adolescent, Physician, Teacher, and School Nurse Views," *Journal of Adolescent Health Care*, 5:254–260, 1984.

Louis Harris and Associates, Sexual Material on American Network Television During the 1987–88 Season, survey conducted for Planned Parenthood Federation of America, Jan. 26, 1988.

Makinson, C., "The Health Consequences of Teenage Fertility," *Family Planning Perspectives*, 17:132–139, 1985.

Marini, M. M., "Sex Differences in Earnings in the United States," *Annual Review of Sociology*, 15:343–380, 1989.

Marsiglio, W. and F. L. Mott, "The Impact of Sex Education on Sexual Activity, Contraceptive Use and Premarital Pregnancy Among American Teenagers," *Family Planning Perspectives*, 18:151–162, 1986.

Martin, T. C. and L. L. Bumpass, "Recent Trends in Marital Disruption," *Demography*, 26:37–51, 1989.

McKinney, D. H. and G. L. Peak, *School-Based and School-Linked Health Centers: Update 1993*, Center for Population Options, Washington, D.C., 1994.

McLaughlin, S. D., D. L. Manninen and L. D. Winges, "Do Adolescents Who Relinquish Their Children Fare Better or Worse Than Those Who Raise Them?" *Family Planning Perspectives*, 20:25–32, 1988.

Moore, K. A., *Facts at a Glance*, Child Trends, Washington, D.C., 1993.

Moore, K. A., C. W. Nord and J. L. Peterson,

"Nonvoluntary Sexual Activity Among Adolescents," *Family Planning Perspectives*, 21:110–114, 1989.

Moore, K. A., C. W. Nord and J. L. Peterson, tabulations of data from the 1987 National Survey of Children, 1993.

Moore, K. A. and T. M. Steif, *Changes in Marriage and Fertility Behavior: Behavior Versus Attitudes of Young Adults*, Child Trends, Washington, D.C., 1989.

Morrison, D. R. and A. J. Cherlin, "The Divorce Process and Young Children's Well-Being: A Prospective Analysis," paper presented at the annual meeting of the Population Association of America, Denver, May 1, 1992.

Moscicki, A. et al., "Differences in Biologic Maturation, Sexual Behavior, and Sexually Transmitted Disease Between Adolescents with and Without Cervical Intraepithelial Neoplasia," *Journal of Pediatrics*, 115:487–493, 1989.

Moscicki, A. et al., "Human Papillomavirus Infection in Sexually Active Adolescent Females: Prevalence and Risk Factors," *Pediatric Research*, 28:507–513, 1990.

Mosher, W. D., "Infertility Trends Among U.S. Couples: 1965–1976," *Family Planning Perspectives*, 14:22–27, 1982.

Moss, A. J. et al., "Recent Trends in Adolescent Smoking, Smoking-Uptake Correlates, and Expectations About the Future," *Advance Data from Vital and Health Statistics*, No. 221, 1992.

Murray, C., "The Coming White Underclass," *Wall Street Journal*, Oct. 29, 1993.

Nathanson, C. A., *Dangerous Passage: The Social Control of Sexuality in Women's Adolescence*, Temple University Press, Philadelphia, 1991.

National Center for Health Statistics (NCHS), *Vital Statistics of the United States, 1965, Vol. I—Natality*, U.S. Government Printing Office, Washington, D.C., 1967.

NCHS, "Advance Report of Final Natality Statistics, 1988," *Monthly Vital Statistics Report*, Vol. 39, No. 4, Supplement, Aug. 15, 1990a.

NCHS, *Vital Statistics of the United States, 1986. Vol. III—Marriage and Divorce*, U.S. Government Printing Office, Washington, D.C., 1990b.

NCHS, *Vital Statistics of the United States, 1988. Vol. II—Mortality. Part A*, U.S. Government Printing Office, Washington, D.C., 1991.

NCHS, "Advance Report of Final Natality Statistics, 1990," *Monthly Vital Statistics Report*, Vol. 41, No. 9, Supplement, Feb. 25, 1993a.

NCHS, "Advance Report of Final Natality Statistics, 1991," *Monthly Vital Statistics Report*, Vol. 42, No. 3, Supplement, Sept. 9, 1993b.

Nicholson, H. J. and L. T. Postrado, "A Comprehensive Age-Phased Approach: Girls Incorporated," in B. C. Miller et al., eds., *Preventing Adolescent Pregnancy*, Sage Publications, Newbury Park, Calif., 1992, pp. 110–138.

Oakley, D., tabulations of data from the University of Michigan Feb. 1987–Apr. 1989 survey on initial clients at three family planning clinics, Detroit, 1993.

Olsen, J. A. et al., "The Effects of Three Abstinence Sex Education Programs on Student Attitudes Toward Sexual Activity," *Adolescence*, 26:631–641, 1991.

Opinion Research Corp., "Teen Sexual Attitudes," prepared for CBS/*Good Housekeeping*, Jan. 5, 1993.

Ostergard, D. R., "The Effect of Age, Gravidity, and Parity on the Location of the Cervical Squamocolumnar Junction as Determined by Colposcopy," *American Journal of Obstetrics and Gynecology*, 129:59–60, 1977.

Osterman, P. *Getting Started: The Youth Labor Market*, MIT Press, Cambridge, Mass., 1980.

Paone, D. and W. Chavkin, "From the Private Family Domain to the Public Health Forum: Sexual Abuse, Women and Risk of HIV Infection," *SIECUS Report*, 21(4):13–16, 1993.

Philliber, S. and J. P. Allen, "Life Options and Community Service: Teen Outreach Program," in B. C. Miller et al., eds., *Preventing Adolescent Pregnancy*, Sage Publications, Newbury Park, Calif., 1992, pp. 139–155.

Pleck, J. H., F. L. Sonenstein and L. C. Ku, "Adolescent Males' Condom Use: Relationships Between Perceived Cost-Benefits and Consistency," *Journal of Marriage and the Family*, 53:733–745, 1991.

Polit, D. F., "Effects of a Comprehensive Program for Teenage Parents: Five Years After Project Redirection," *Family Planning Perspectives*, 21:164–169, 187, 1989.

Polit, D. F. and J. R. Kahn, "Early Subsequent Pregnancy Among Economically Disadvantaged Teenage Mothers," *American Journal of Public Health*, 76:167–171, 1986.

Rabin, J. M., V. Seltzer and S. Pollack, "The Benefits of a Comprehensive Teenage Pregnancy Program," *American Journal of Gynecologic Health*, 6(3):66–74, 1992.

Ralph, N. and A. Edgington, "An Evaluation of an Adolescent Family Planning Program," *Journal of Adolescent Health Care*, 4:158–162, 1983.

Randall, T., "Adolescents May Experience Home, School Abuse; Their Future Draws Researchers' Concern," *Journal of the American Medical Association*, 267:3127–3131, 1992.

Reiss, I. L. "Sexual Pluralism: Ending America's Sexual Crisis," *SIECUS Report*, 19(3):5–9, 1991.

Roper, W. L., H. B. Peterson and J. W. Curran, "Commentary: Condoms and HIV/STD Prevention—Clarifying the Message," *American Journal of Public Health*, 83:501–503, 1990.

Saluter, A. F., "Marital Status and Living Arrangements, March 1991," *Current Population Reports*, Series P-20, No. 461, 1992.

Saracco, A. et al., "Man-to-Woman Sexual Transmission of HIV: Longitudinal Study of 343 Steady Partners of Infected Men," *Journal of Acquired Immune Deficiency Syndromes*, 6:497–502, 1993.

Schachter, J., "Why We Need a Program for the Control of Chlamydia Trachomatis," *New England Journal of Medicine*, 320:802–804, 1989.

Shafer, M. and R. L. Sweet, "Pelvic Inflammatory Disease in Adolescent Females," *Adolescent Medicine: State of the Art Reviews*, 1:545–564, 1990.

Silverman, J. and A. Torres, *Barriers to Contraceptive Services*, AGI, New York, 1987.

Singh, S., J. D. Forrest and A. Torres, *Prenatal Care in the United States: A State and County Inventory, Vol. 1*, AGI, New York, 1989.

Smith, T. W., "A Methodological Review of Sexual Behavior Questions on the 1988 and 1989 GSS," *GSS Methodological Report*, No. 65, National Opinion Research Center, Chicago, 1988.

Sonenstein, F. L., J. H. Pleck and L. C. Ku, "Sexual Activity, Condom Use and AIDS Awareness Among Adolescent Males," *Family Planning Perspectives*, 21:152–158, 1989.

Sonenstein, F. L., J. H. Pleck and L. C. Ku, "Levels of Sexual Activity Among Adolescent Males in the United States," *Family Planning Perspectives*, 23:162–167, 1991.

Steinberg, L. "Jumping Off the Work Experience

Bandwagon," *Journal of Youth and Adolescence,* **11:**183–205, 1982.

Stipp, H., "New Ways to Reach Children," *American Demographics,* Aug. 1993, pp. 50–56.

Stout, J. W., and F. P. Rivara, "Schools and Sex Education: Does It Work?" *Pediatrics,* 83:375–379, 1989.

Tanfer, K., tabulations of data from the 1991 National Survey of Men, 1993.

Thomson, E., S. S. McLanahan and R. B. Curtin, "Family Structure, Gender and Parental Socialization," *Journal of Marriage and the Family,* 54:368–378, 1992.

Torres, A. and J. D. Forrest, "Why Do Women Have Abortions?" *Family Planning Perspectives,* 20:169–176, 1988.

Trent, K. and S. J. South, "Sociodemographic Status, Parental Background, Childhood Family Structure, and Attitudes Toward Family Formation," *Journal of Marriage and the Family,* 54:427–439, 1992.

Trudell, B. and M. Whatley, "Sex Respect: A Problematic Public School Sexuality Curriculum," *Journal of Sex Education and Therapy,* 17:125–140, 1991.

Udry, J. R. and J. O. G. Billy, "Initiation of Coitus in Early Adolescence," *American Sociological Review,* 52:841–855, 1987.

U.S. Bureau of the Census, "Poverty in the United States: 1987," *Current Population Reports,* Series P-60, No. 163, 1989.

U.S. Bureau of the Census, "United States Population Estimates, by Age, Sex, Race, and Hispanic Origin, 1980–1988," *Current Population Reports,* Series P-25, No. 1045, 1990.

U.S. Bureau of the Census, "Marital Status and Living Arrangements: March, 1990," *Current Population Reports,* Series P-20, No. 450, 1991.

U.S. Bureau of the Census, *Statistical Abstract of the United States: 1992,* U.S. Government Printing Office, Washington, D.C., 1992.

U.S. Congress, Office of Technology Assessment, *Adolescent Health—Vol. II: Background and the Effectiveness of Selected Prevention and Treatment Services,* U.S. Government Printing Office, Washington, D.C., 1991.

Upchurch, D. M. and J. McCarthy, "The Timing of First Birth and High School Completion," *American Sociological Review,* 55:224–234, 1990.

Vincent, M. L., A. F. Clearie and M. D. Schluchter, "Reducing Adolescent Pregnancy Through School and Community-Based Education," *Journal of the American Medical Association,* 257:3382–3386, 1987.

Wallace, H. M., J. Weeks and A. Medina, "Services for Pregnant Teenagers in the Large Cities of the United States, 1970–1980," *Journal of the American Medical Association,* 248:2270–2273, 1982.

Walter, H. J. and R. D. Vaughn, "AIDS Risk Reduction Among a Multiethnic Sample of Urban High School Students," *Journal of the American Medical Association,* 270:725–762, 1993.

Warrick, L. et al., "Educational Outcomes in Teenage Pregnancy and Parenting Programs: Results from a Demonstration," *Family Planning Perspectives,* 25:148–155, 1993.

Wasserheit, J. N., "Epidemiological Synergy: Interrelationship Between Human Immunodeficiency Virus Infection and Other Sexually Transmitted Diseases," *Sexually Transmitted Diseases,* 19:61–77, 1992.

Wilson, W. J., *The Truly Disadvantaged,* University of Chicago Press, Chicago, 1987.

Winter, L. and L. Breckenmaker, "Tailoring Family Planning Services to the Special Needs of Adolescents," *Family Planning Perspectives,* 23:24–30, 1991.

Wu, L. L. and B. C. Martinson, "Family Structure and the Risk of a Premarital Birth," *American Sociological Review,* 58:210–232, 1993.

Zabin, L. S., "School-Linked Health Services: The Johns Hopkins Program," in B. C. Miller et al., eds., *Preventing Adolescent Pregnancy,* Sage Publications, Newbury Park, Calif., 1992, pp. 156–184.

Zabin, L. S., M. B. Hirsch and J. A. Boscia, "Differential Characteristics of Adolescent Pregnancy Test Patients: Abortion, Childbearing and Negative Test Groups," *Care,* 11:107–113, 1990.

Zabin, L. S. et al., "Evaluation of a Pregnancy Prevention Program for Urban Teenagers," *Family Planning Perspectives,* 18:119–126, 1986.

Zellman, G. L., "Public School Programs for Adolescent Pregnancy and Parenthood: An Assessment," *Family Planning Perspectives,* 14:15–21, 1982.

Zelnik, M. and Y. J. Kim, "Sex Education and Its Association with Teenage Sexual Activity, Pregnancy and Contraceptive Use," *Family Planning Perspectives,* 14:117–125, 1982.

Zierler, S. et al., "Adult Survivors of Childhood Sexual Abuse and Subsequent Risk of HIV Infection," *American Journal of Public Health,* 81:572–575, 1991.

Copy Editor: Dore Hollander
Production Manager: Kathleen Randall
Senior Production Assistants: Jessica Black,
Paul Blaser
Production Assistants: Pouchine Joseph,
Scott Klein
Design: Emerson Wajdowicz Studios, Inc.
Printing: BSC Litho